Feeling Your Way Through Life

David De Notaris

insight *i* publishing group

Tulsa, Oklahoma

Feeling Your Way Through Life

Feeling Your Way Through Life by David De Notaris
Published by Insight Publishing Group
8801 S. Yale, Suite 410
Tulsa, OK 74137
918-493-1718

Cover design by Jeffery Mobley

ISBN 1-930027-34-6
Library of Congress catalog card number: 2001087529

Printed in the United States of America

David De Notaris Seminars
www.daviddenotaris.com
(877) tap-hope (827-4773)
Fax: (973) 239-0932
"Do You Have A Minute?"
Daily Motivational Hotline: (973) 571-0999
Email: david@daviddenotaris.com

Table of Contents

Introduction

When I was young, I was diagnosed with a rare eye condition called Retinitis Pigmentosa (RP). According to the doctors, the future would be bleak: total blindness by age twenty.

Even though I had a visual impairment, my parents gave me every opportunity to lead a "normal" life. One afternoon when I was eight, my father called me from work. He said, "David, when I come home from work, I am going to teach you how to play catch." I was never so afraid. I couldn't see a baseball, football, or softball, and I didn't want to get hurt.

My father realized this and focused on what I could see: contrast (light on dark). That day he brought home a beach ball. It was so big that I couldn't get my arms around it. My father hit the beach ball up in the air, and I was able to see the red, yellow, blue, and green against the light blue sky. I was able to catch the ball!

Nothing felt better than playing catch with my dad! My father told me that day, "David, I am not teaching you just how to play catch; I am teaching you that you can do anything you want. You just have to figure out how!"

Feeling Your Way Through Life is filled with insights, stories, and ideas that will help you figure out how to lead a more satisfying, happy, and fulfilling life. Good luck. God bless your continued success.

Part I
Feeling

1 Feeling Your Way Through Life

I was born with the rare eye disorder Retinitis Pigmentosa (RP), which is a degenerative condition that leaves scarring on the retina. This disorder first causes night blindness, then the loss of peripheral vision (the ability to see on the side of you), and sometimes it can even cause total blindness. When I was four-years-old, my parents took me to a specialist for an exam. They suspected that I had a vision problem, because my older sister Jerilyn had a similar disorder. The doctors did not give my parents much hope and advised them to enroll me in a school for the blind. My parents declined taking the doctor's advice and enrolled me in Belleville Public School in Belleville, New Jersey, which is about fifteen miles west of New York City.

As a youngster, I wouldn't have even known I had a problem, if it weren't for listening to the doctor's conversation with my parents. I remember listening to my father as he rifled questions at the unsympathetic doctor: "What about surgery? What about glasses? What about treatments?" My father was rudely interrupted by the doctor, who replied, "Mr. De Notaris, your son is blind, and there is nothing you can do about it."

That comment couldn't have been further from the truth. There is always something you can do about any problem, even if it is just changing your perspective on how you feel about the problem. I was told that blindness would beat me or that I would beat it-the choice was mine. Now, some twenty-six years later, I realize that everyone has problems and crosses to bear. I once heard someone say, "If you have a pulse, you have a problem-what are you going to do with yours? Is it going to beat you, or will you, with a powerful support group, beat it?"

I began feeling my way through life when my mother began teaching me the alphabet with magnetic letters on the refrigerator. She taught me words such as mom, dad, pop, and so on. I learned what numbers are, what my name feels like, and what my brothers' and sisters' names feel like through touch. My world was opening up because someone took the time to make me feel like everyone else: normal.

My parents spent time figuring out which toys would help a blind child. Legos helped me learn how to build things I could touch when the other kids were drawing what they could see. They bought me games with big bright lights so that I could see the contrast. They made it their job to help me fit in. As I learned later in life, they were also feeling their way through the situation. They had no support groups, no expert advisers-they just had their simple common sense to lead the way.

I can vividly remember my first few days of school. My father showed me where the water fountain, bathrooms, bookshelves, and chairs were. He made it comfortable for me to be involved. I was asked if I was scared, but I wasn't smart enough at that point to be scared. I'm sure there were a lot of people who were nervous about how I would handle public school.

I remember one night that one of my parents' friends asked my father, "What blind school does David go to?"

My father replied proudly, "Oh, David goes to a regular school; it's called mainstreamed." That was the first time I had ever heard the term mainstreamed, but it followed me through my educational career. I was in regular classes, and sometimes I didn't know how I was going to manage. But that was okay.

Not knowing how to do something should never be a reason for not doing it. When we don't know how to do something, it is a simple test of our imagination and our ability to feel our way through something. It's the opportunity to call upon a greater power. I call this power God; you can call it whatever you'd like. It's the time to call upon friends, family, and support groups to help you make the right decisions. These are the turning points in our lives. We can talk ourselves out of something or into something.

I recall being in first grade and going to a little convenience store next to my school. The owner's name was Harry. One day I went to the store with my friend to buy some bubble gum, red hots, and football cards. (I believe the purchase came to thirty-two cents.) Football and baseball cards used to be wrapped in clear plastic so that you could see the top card and read the bottom card in the pack. I remember that before I picked out the football cards I was going to buy, Harry told me which teams were on the top of the football cards he was selling.

He said, "David, there is a Minnesota Viking, a Denver Bronco, and a Dallas Cowboy."

My friend asked, "Why are you reading him the cards?"

Harry replied, "He deserves to have the same opportunity that you have, and he deserves to have a choice like everyone else. You should help him the same way."

Why this man, a convenience store owner, was concerned with my rights, I'll never know. Harry, wherever you are, thank you for giving me the opportunity to lead a normal life. I am sure Harry never had accessibility training or anything like that; he was just another caring person helping me feel my way through life.

I would take my football cards or baseball cards home, and my mother or father or brothers and sisters would read me the players' names, the names of the teams they played on, and their positions. I didn't really care about the players or the teams, but I enjoyed the time I shared with my family.

We can measure many things, but the time that families and communities invest in children is invaluable. Giving kids a sense of fitting in, of feeling good about themselves, and giving them the opportunities to succeed and fail will really prepare kids for life ahead.

2 Feeling Your Way Through Love

I thought I knew what romantic love was in high school when I was going to the prom. I thought I knew what love was when I had my first serious relationship in college. I thought I knew what love was when I went out with a girl in college who was everything I thought I wanted. I thought I knew what love was when I was told I was loved by all of them, but speaking of love isn't love. It is the consistent showing of love that proves it. Anyone can speak words, and anyone can think they love someone. But it is the love of someone who stays with you, the love of someone who believes in you, that is the true definition of love.

I experienced this love with my wife, Mariann. Mariann was born on December 8, 1969, in Atlanta, Georgia, exactly eight weeks after I was born. Who knew when I met her at a Super Bowl party that she would change my world forever? I met Mariann at my fraternity house in January of 1990.

I heard a commotion near the basement steps and went to find out what was going on. Mariann was carrying on her back another girl down the steps. They were both small girls, and I was wondering what this was all about. I thought it was one of those sorority things. The girls were Mariann and her friend Paula. I said to Mariann, "Why are you carrying that girl down the steps?"

She replied, "My friend Paula has CP, and it's hard for her to walk down the steps with the crowd.

So I helped her. Are you all right with that? And may I have something to drink? It's hot in here."

I was intrigued by someone who was twenty-years-old and was not concerned about her image of helping someone. Many times people are so concerned with their image that they are too afraid to help, but not Mariann. Mariann and I had a great time talking and laughing that night. We were in the same major: speech communications. Mariann had just transferred from a college in Philadelphia. I really didn't see Mariann around too much after that, not until March when one of my friends, Rick Bowman, told me he was going out with one of Mariann's friends' roommates. He asked me if I wanted her number.

The next time I saw Mariann was at Phi Sigma Kappa's St. Patrick's Day party. Mariann is half Irish and half Italian, and she loves St. Patrick's Day. We started spending more time together, and I called Mariann from Daytona, Florida, over spring break.

Mariann had the ability to fit in wherever we went, from meetings with the president of the college to fraternity parties, and it was a pleasure to be with her. We liked each other's friends and even each other's families. We enjoyed the same music and the same food, and we both loved to laugh and have fun. I remember Mariann's first gift to me; it was a laughing box. She said she wanted me to have it because if she wasn't there to make me laugh she thought the laughing box could.

I met Mariann's family in October of 1990, and was I terrified. I had met other girlfriends' parents, but none of them really liked me. Looking back on it, it didn't really matter because I didn't like them either. I realized why Mariann's family was so special; her family was just like her. I felt accepted, and for me that felt good. I never felt like "Dave the Blind Guy" or felt less than what other people had tried to make me feel.

I remember one girlfriend told me that her father said, "Why are you going out with a blind guy? He can't take care of himself. How is he going to take care of you?" Those things hurt. It's not what the parent said that bothered me. What bothered me was that someone who had known me for a few months still thought that was true.

I have always made efforts to take care of myself and even to help take care of others. I am always trying to help other people excel. I believe people who love us help give us answers and not more questions. They show us how to do something; they don't ask us how we are going to do something. Love is supportive, encouraging, and liberating, not confining. Friends see us through rather than say we're through.

Mariann taught me how to cook, live, and even dream when other people asked, "How are you going to do that?" Mariann would say, "How about trying it like this? Have you ever thought of trying it this way?"

Love brings a can-do attitude, and that's what drives me to this day. I put my God and my family first. Mariann has always had the ability to encourage, to polish, and to make everything right, and that is what makes my world go 'round.

3 Feeling Your Way Through with Faith

Faith is the most important key to all successes. I have read hundreds of books, journals, and magazines; attended hundreds of seminars; and listened to thousands of hours of tapes of speakers. The common thread that links them all is a theory from the Bible, and that is faith. Many people try to sugarcoat it and say it's the universe or a greater power that makes us successful, but I know without a shadow of a doubt that faith is the key. Faith is risking it all on something unseen. Most people say, "I'll believe it when I see it," but the truth of the matter is that you'll see it when you believe it.

Growing up blind, I have had great faith in God. My parents took my entire family to church every Sunday. I believe this truly shaped my life for the better, and today my wife and I attend church with our family. A verse in the Bible that I am sure you have heard tells us to walk by faith, not by sight (2 Cor. 5:7). This verse has always spoken to me. It has really hit home because if I always walked by sight, I would not go anywhere.

When we act with faith in our lives and in our hearts, we aren't acting irresponsibly; we believe that things are going to work out. I've heard it said,

"Things work out the best for people who make the best of the way things work out."

I remember my father telling me one time I would have to walk home from elementary school. "What are you afraid of?" he asked. I told him I was afraid of all the people and all the cars. My father gave me a kernel of hope that has never left me. He said, "David, if you knew who walked in front of you, beside you, and behind you, you would never be afraid. You have guardian angels that will protect you in whatever situation you go through."

I have been lost in different places: train stations, schools, and stores. But I have remembered that quote, and it put me at ease. As soon as we stop worrying, a solution pops up. If we put our energy in worrying, that is what we will harvest. If we put our energy in faith, that will grow as well.

Faith is just like a muscle, and we have to exercise it, even flex it. Sometimes we have to flex it in difficult situations. We must remember that God doesn't pay all His bills on Tuesday at ten o'clock, and sometimes we have to wait until Thursday or maybe even the following week. But God will always give an answer. It will probably not come in the form of a booming voice. Notice I say *will probably not* because it may, but the answer will come to you when you're waiting in faith for an answer. It may come to you while reading, walking, swimming, or even sleeping, but the answer will come.

I remember needing surgery on my cataract. According to the doctors, it needed to be done; however, it was not a simple procedure. After some discussion with my wife and other doctors, I agreed to the procedure. I was concerned about the surgery but was hopeful that it would restore some of my vision.

I was in the hospital being prepared for the surgery, and Mariann was sitting at my side when the doctor entered the room. "David," he said, "you are scheduled for one o'clock." My stomach got tight, and I felt a lump in my throat.

"What will happen?" I asked.

"You will get a needle in your eye to stabilize it." I was too shocked to say anything. He patted me on the shoulder and said, "David, everything will be fine." Then he quickly left the room. I didn't say anything, and a few seconds later Mariann started laughing.

"What are you laughing at?" I barked.

"You're going to get a needle in your eye." Mariann has always had the wonderful ability to make people feel comfortable in uncomfortable situations. "You're going to be fine," Mariann said as she kissed me on my cheek.

I never felt the needle, and then I was in the operating room. I was able to respond and even ask questions to the doctors and staff in the room. The surgery was at a teaching hospital, so I was able to listen to the doctor make observations to the intern. I remember hearing the doctor quietly say, "There is too much blood here."

This got me concerned, but the thought my father had planted in my head twenty years before came to mind: "If you knew who walked with you, you would fear nothing." Then I was able to see in my mind's eye a group of soldiers standing against the wall.

I asked, "Who are they?"

I heard a calm yet strong voice respond, "They are angels."

"What are they doing?" I silently asked.

"They are watching the doctor." I felt a great sense of peace that I had never before experienced. I imagine that some of you may be skeptical when reading this; I also would be if it hadn't happened to me.

Faith believes in things unseen. People have asked me to "prove there is a supernatural God." My response is "Prove to me there isn't." When we walk by faith, we see things we never could imagine.

Part II
Living

4 Fighting Destroys Ambition.

One of my favorite words in the world is harmony. Even as I am typing this on my portable note taker with speech output, the word *harmony* sounds happy. What comes to mind when you think of the word *harmony?* I think of being in Disney World and hearing "It's a small world". Harmony is fun, and it feels good as well.

Harmony and peace go together like a hand and a glove. When there is harmony or peace in a family, office, or organization, many miracles happen before our eyes. People do things for each other, not because they have to but because they get to. Harmony creates ambition. It creates an environment in which people can work together to create, develop, and devise their plans and dreams.

Fighting destroys ambition. It takes away creativity. Bickering creates a hollow feeling inside, and it makes people feel lonely and afraid. It makes a hard-working man or woman stay at work, not to work but to stay away from the constant poking, picking, and insulting.

I remember a relationship in which I was picked on in a battle of discouragements. I lived for the ten to fifteen seconds of peace that rarely came. I was doing my best to make her happy, but it never seemed to work. That brings me to my next point: People don't just fight with others, but they fight with themselves as well.

Do you talk to yourself? When I ask that question, people pause and say to themselves, "Do I talk to myself? Hm, I don't think so." We all talk to ourselves. Science proves we have over fifteen hundred thoughts per minute. And studies show it is possible that eighty percent of these thoughts are negative. We must have harmony in ourselves. We must feel good about who we are and about the people we are becoming every day.

I have found that when I am working out four days per week for just thirty to forty-five minutes, I feel better, not bitter. My clothes fit better, and I have a mental edge on the rest of the world. When I don't exercise, I can't let go of the things that are on my mind, and I can't free the negative energy and negative calories. However, when I exercise, the negative energy is let go, and my head is clear. I can concentrate on my dreams, not on my downfalls.

Harmony is something we must have with others, but it must start inside us first. Our outside world is a direct result of our inside world. If there is no harmony on the inside, there will be none on the outside.

Here are a few tips for bringing harmony:

1.   When you wake up, say, "Good morning, God!" Don't say, "Good God, morning!"

2.   Whisper this prayer: "Good morning, God. What are you up to today? Whatever it is, please count me in!"

3.   Spend five to seven minutes going over your day. This little technique will stop you from

forgetting what you have to do and keep you from falling all over yourself.

4.   Keep a day planner. Trying to hold onto uncompleted tasks is fatiguing, and it is hard to have harmony when we are mentally exhausted.

Harmony is like singing angels; life is sweet, peaceful, and fulfilling. Let's get harmony on the inside, and we will positively change our worlds on the outside! Harmony not only sounds good, but it feels even better.

5 Our Decisions Determine Our Destiny.

Did you ever hear the story about the man at his retirement party? After all the speeches, kind words, and gifts, a younger employee asked the retiree his secret to success in running the company. The retiree replied, "Making good decisions."

"How do you learn to make good decisions?" asked the young man.

"By making bad decisions and learning from them."

Many times we make decisions based on feelings alone. I know this book is on feeling your way through life, but when our feelings are not healthy, positive, and motivating, we must be cautious. I am sure there has been at least one night when you woke up to go to the bathroom and couldn't go back to sleep. You started thinking about all the things going

David De Notaris

on at work and at home. You started wondering why this was happening to you. Maybe you had reasons for why some of these things were happening to you, and five seconds or five minutes later you were feeling sorry for yourself.

The mind is a dangerous thing if we let it wander. If we allow every thought to float in, plant itself, and grow, we will drive ourselves crazy. We have the ability to decide what thoughts we are going to dwell on.

When I was growing up, I used to worry about what other kids thought about my thick glasses. Then I came to the conclusion that no one really cared about my glasses because they were too worried about their own situation. We cannot always base our decisions on how we feel at any particular moment. I learned the H.A.L.T. method. Never make a decision when you are Hungry, Angry, Lonely, or Tired.

When you are hungry, angry, lonely, or tired, you are making decisions strictly on feelings, not on facts. We must make decisions using all the information around us, not just based on the information within us. I have found that some of my best decisions, plans, and thoughts have come to me while I was praying, meditating, or just thinking on the treadmill. It is simply amazing when we get in motion how we can clear our brains and allow positive, healthy thoughts to drop from heaven into our lives. It is a pleasure to exercise our bodies to clear our minds.

I remember one day a gentleman on the phone told me that blind people don't live as long as sighted

26

people due to all the stress and struggles blind people have to put up with. I was scared and nervous, and I didn't know what to think. I was even too embarrassed to tell anyone else because I was afraid of what they would think. I went to the gym and got on the treadmill to work out. After twenty to twenty-five minutes, the worries seemed ridiculous, even silly. I heard a long time ago that stagnant water stinks; that is why we have to get in motion and stay in motion. Our motions can change our moods and can even change our minds.

When we are in motion—being not just busy but productive—things start to change around us, and change is what this book is really about. We have the ability to change our minds and then in turn change our lives. My hope is that you will not just make decisions based on how you are feeling at a particular time. Make decisions based on the facts that lie around you. Logic cannot change feelings, but feelings can change the way you look at your world.

We must remember the law of inertia: Things in motion stay in motion, and things at rest stay at rest unless acted upon by a greater force. If you're not moving, you must get moving. If you are moving in the wrong direction, you must stop and get moving in the right direction.

We must remember that our beliefs can change our behaviors, our actions can change our attitudes, and our motions can change our moods.

6 Random Acts of Kindness—on Purpose

On my thirty-first birthday, Mariann said she wanted to take me out for lunch. She asked where I wanted to go. I suggested Johnny's Pizza II in West Orange. So off we went. Frank, the owner, had my favorite kind of pizza: cheese-steak. Frank asked me why my wife was with me for lunch. I had been going to Johnny's Pizza for eight years but never with Mariann. I explained that it was my thirty-first birthday on Friday. Frank wished me a happy birthday and handed me our slices. Mariann and I had a nice lunch, and then I went to the counter to pay. To this day I cannot figure out how Mariann took me out for lunch, and I paid.

While Mariann and I were walking out to the car, she handed me a cake box. She said that Frank had handed it to her after I paid. Frank had asked her to give it to me and to say it was from her. In the box was my favorite dessert: strawberry cheesecake. It made my day because someone took time out of their day and went out of their way to make someone feel special.

We often focus on the big things: the cars, the house, the bank account, and the portfolio. But little things mean a lot. Little is more flattering than someone's remembering your name, your birthday, that you love tomatoes, or that you are allergic to strawberries. It's the little things that we remember that let people know we care.

I remember meeting Dr. Kenneth Jernigan, president imaratese National Federation of the Blind. I met him at a conference in Princeton, New Jersey. Dr. Jernigan was totally blind and spoke about the potential of people who are blind. I was so moved by his presentation that I stood in a line of a couple hundred people to meet him.

I was really inspired by his presentation but even more so by meeting him. I said, "Dr. Jernigan, my name is David De Notaris, and it is a pleasure to personally meet you." What happened next blew my mind.

He said, "David De Notaris, please spell De Notaris." So I spelled it for him, and then he spelled it back to me and said, "That is a name with character. I'll never forget it." He took the time—maybe fifteen to twenty seconds—to learn the correct spelling. Again, it is the little things that people remember that give people an internal smile.

When I make presentations, I ask people if an elephant has ever bitten them. Most of the time people say no. But everyone has been bitten by a mosquito. It's the little things that get us. It's the little decisions that we make day by day that determine the quality of our lives; make the decision to improve something today!

7 How to Make Yourself Younger

When flipping through stations on the radio or television, surfing the Internet, or browsing the local newspaper, we are bound to find some moisturizer cream or lotion that will bring us back to yesteryear. Then things were easier, problems were fewer, and life was, oh, so simple. Miracle creams and lotions are fine to rejuvenate our skin, but I believe that getting back to our childhood is deeper than skin.

Thinking of my childhood brings me back to when all my brothers and sisters were home, when we all sat down for dinner together. I can even smell my mother's tomato sauce. Garden-picked tomatoes, fresh basil, and crushed garlic produce the smell of Sunday morning at the De Notaris household. Every Sunday afternoon at two, my entire family would sit down for a family dinner, which usually included macaroni, meatballs, Italian bread, and freshly grated cheese. To this day, when I bring my son David to my mother's home after church, the smell of tomato sauce fills the room and brings me back twenty-five years.

I believe we can keep ourselves young by surrounding ourselves with the things that make us feel young. Pine-scented candles work for me. I think of Christmas, when my mother would wrap a Christmas gift on the dining room table and say, "This is for your brother. Be careful now, and put it under the tree." The smell of pine brings me back to a time of love and joy.

What are the smells that bring you back to when problems were simple, worries were unheard of, and life's focus was backyard fun? Think about what brings you back to the good memories, the fun times, and the times when playing was your job.

Do not *just* look to the past for the good memories. I get angry when people say, "Those were the good old days." These are the good days! There are more opportunities now than ever before. So answer this question: What are the sounds, smells, sights, and tastes that help you think of where you are right now? Remember to also look at the present and the future. Design new traditions for your family to someday fondly look back on and smile at.

8 Sleeping in Heavenly Peace

Nothing feels as good as a good night's sleep. When we wake up, we are rested, rejuvenated, and ready to take on the world. When we have things on our mind, we wake up at three in the morning and worry about everything: work, bills, the big client, the account, the boss, the report, the secretary, the game. I have found that the following exercise has helped me clear my mind and have an enjoyable night. I like to, as the song says, "sleep in heavenly peace."

I do this exercise on Sunday evening before bed and review it early Monday morning. I call it the ten-minute drill. For ten minutes I look at the areas of my life. Take the time to answer these questions. Answering them always helps free me. Father of Psychology William James said, "Nothing is more fatiguing than holding onto the uncompleted task." Stop holding onto all the things you want to do, have to do, or need to do. Complete this exercise and feel free.

1.   Health. How am I feeling? What will I be eating? What exercise will I be doing?
2.   Family. How are the people around me? Is anyone having problems that need help, success that needs praising, or concerns that need addressing?
3.   Friends. Who haven't I talked to lately? Who has been on my mind?
4.   Work. What project must I work on? What information do I need? Who must I contact?
5.   Community. What is going on around my family? How can I help?
6.   Church. What programs, trips, or lectures are going on that I should be involved with or attend?
7.   Inspiration. What information can I read or listen to that will get me closer to my dreams?
8.   Relaxation. What can I do this week to help me get centered and make me feel great?

Don't just read these questions, but take a few minutes to answer them. These questions revolve around the four key areas of life: physical, mental, emotional, and spiritual. If we are running on two or three cylinders, we are not working or living to our fullest potential. We must make sure that all the areas are fully functioning. When all of our internal components are operating, we feel strong, confident, and satisfied. Then we believe we can handle anything that comes our way.

I once heard a priest explain that he had spent hundreds of hours with people on their deathbeds. He went on to say that not one of them ever said, "I wish I spent more time at the office," but all of them talked about birthday parties, picnics, and special times with their families. Take a look at all the areas of your life so that you can feel strong and healthy.

Ben Franklin said that if you think an education is expensive, try ignorance.

9 The Truth About Lying

Much of the stress people encounter is derived from dishonesty. People first lie to themselves and then to others. I remember growing up and hearing someone say, "It's just a little white lie, no big deal" or "It's just a little fib." Little lies and baby fibs grow up to become full-grown lies.

L.I.E.S. leave individuals extremely sad.

One day a little boy was telling mean and nasty lies about his friend. The little boy who told the lies confessed to his grandfather. Then he asked, "Grandfather, what should I do?"

His grandfather paused and then said, "Go and fetch my feather pillow." The boy quickly and nervously ran to fetch Grandfather's pillow.

"Here it is, Grandpa."

"Okay, now take it outside, open it up, and get all the feathers out."

It was a chilly fall day, and the wind was really blowing. The little boy took Grandfather's feather pillow out back. The boy opened the pillow, and the feathers started blowing everywhere. The little boy watched as the feathers blew in every direction. He then returned to tell his grandfather that he was finished.

Grandfather said, "Fine, now go outside and try to collect the feathers."

The little boy insisted, "It would be impossible to collect all those feathers, Grandfather."

"That's correct. They're just like your lies; you can never collect them either," said Grandfather.

There are at least two problems with telling lies. First, you have to have a great memory to remember the lies you tell. Second, car thieves always lock their car, forgers never leave their signature hanging around, and people who tell lies cannot trust anyone.

Telling the truth cleans the soul and feels good. A wise person once said, "When you tell the truth, you don't have to worry about what you've said." When we are honest with others and ourselves, the world is a happier, more peaceful, and better place to live.

10 Laughing Your Way to Health

Nothing feels as good as when you are with family or old friends, laughing about old times and making new memories to laugh about in the future. Many doctors believe that seventy-seven to eighty-five percent of the illnesses in this world come from stress and worry. We let external circumstances dictate how we feel and what we do. We must be aware of our feelings and have the ability to laugh at things and at ourselves.

When I was dating Mariann, she was living in Havertown, a suburb of Philadelphia. I was living in Montclair, New Jersey. On Friday afternoons, Mariann would drive up to visit, or I would take the train from Penn Station Newark.

It was a hot and busy Friday, and I just made the 6:03 train. I was carrying my computer bag, my duffel bag, and my white cane. The train was extremely crowded; it was standing room only, and people were elbow to elbow. The train started moving, and as the train shook and moved around curves, people would lean into each other. It was very hot, and the train's air-conditioning was not working. I was still in my suit from work. As you could probably imagine, I've had better days.

I decided that I wasn't going to let these external circumstances get me down. Happiness comes from within, not from without. I decided that I was going to start smiling. Smiling is inertia for the soul and can get our attitude moving in a positive direction. I really didn't feel like smiling. I was hot and uncomfortable, and people were shoving. It was just a long day. I said, "Okay, I am going to smile." I hadn't been smiling.

Five seconds later, a man standing in front of me put down his newspaper and abruptly asked, "What the hell are you smiling at?" I was shocked. I didn't know what to say. After a couple of seconds, which felt like a couple of hours at the time, I explained that I was going to see my girlfriend, and I wasn't going to let this situation bother me.

He was standing maybe twelve inches from me and said, "Buddy, are all blind people as crazy as you are?" Again, I didn't know what to say. I just stood there numb. My father taught me that you don't always have to get the last word, so I didn't say anything.

After a few stops, most of the people got off the train, and there were some open seats. I sat down, wondering about what had just happened a few minutes before, and I started to laugh. Then my stop came, so I gathered my bags. The train door opened, and there was Mariann. It was great to see her. During the car ride to her home, I told her the story. I wasn't really sure if I should be upset or what. Mariann started laughing hysterically and said, "That is a great story. Imagine what kind of day that guy must have had."

I thought about it, and she was right. Mariann said, "You just have to look and see humor in some situations." We can sit around and wonder why some things happen, why people say what they say, but we must have a light heart and learn to laugh at ourselves and at crazy situations.

There is a song that says, "You'll have a head start if you are among the very young at heart." We must remember that problems happen to everyone. We can choose whether the situation makes us bitter or better. Have a song in your heart and love in your voice. Have the ability to see the beauty and joy of life. If we do these things, our lives will be filled with peace, joy, and happiness.

Part III
Helping

11 Can Things We Hate Help Us the Most?

I believe the answer to this question is a big, fat yes. One of the things I know everyone dislikes that can springboard us is the feeling of dissatisfaction. I believe if we can get in touch with our dissatisfaction, we can have a great starting point for change. I guess we should first identify what dissatisfaction feels like.

Dissatisfaction feels like "There's got to be more than this." I remember being in first grade and having the doctors tell my parents that there were some special glasses that would make it possible for me to read. I remember sitting in class in the row closest to the window because the light from the window made it easier for me to see. One of my classmates said, "You are so lucky. You can't read this book, and you don't have to do the same work."

I remember telling him, "Not for long. My father is bringing me special glasses that will allow me to read." I remember being able to see lines on the page with little spaces between them, later to find out those were the words and not lines like I had first thought. My father came into school with the new glasses, walked into the classroom, and brought them to my desk. It was not a special production, and I don't think anyone was watching because the students were too busy doing their work.

My father came over to me and said, "David, put these on." I got so excited. This was it. I was going to be like everyone else. I would be able to read. I put the glasses on, started looking at the words, and saw nothing. The words were not bigger, the pictures weren't clearer, and I still couldn't see. I guess my father saw the look of disappointment or dissatisfaction on my face. "Here, David, look at the picture, not the words. Can you tell me what that is?" I just shook my head no. He put his hand on my shoulder, stood up, and said, "I'll talk to you at dinner." I guess he was as disappointed as I was and maybe even more so.

I am not sure what happened behind the scenes, but I heard him talking to the teacher in the hallway. I wish I knew exactly what they said, but a few minutes later Ms. Higgins came over to me and whispered, "Everything is going to be all right."

That day I got my first real taste of dissatisfaction. I guess all I wanted was to be like everyone else, and that was not going to happen. Dissatisfaction drove me to change. I didn't realize it at the time, but I was resisting learning Braille. This dissatisfaction with not being able to read drove my parents and me to take on the challenge of Braille. Braille is a series of six dots read with one's fingers. Once I learned Braille, I also learned how to read. Today, embrace dissatisfaction and see where it drives you, your family, your company, and your school.

I thought the other students wouldn't like me because they were reading print, and I was reading Braille. Little did I know that my teachers had another plan. I made many friends by explaining and teaching Braille to my classmates. This activity opened the doors of communication between the other students and me.

People say children are cruel, but I never had that experience. I guess the worst thing one of my own classmates did was put banana bubble gum on my seat. At the time, it felt pretty bad; I felt pretty foolish. Looking back on it, I guess it was pretty silly. Actually, it made me feel like one of the guys. Everyone at one time or another had gum put on their seat. When I was leaving the class at the end of the day, my teacher said to me, "David, don't be upset about the gum on your seat. Everyone gets a chance to be laughed at." She turned my dissatisfaction into peace with a little thought.

Dissatisfaction can be the driving force to change. If you don't like the way something is or feels, you can change it. The first thing we must change is the way we are looking at the problem. I remember being told, "It's not the problem but how you handle the problem that really matters." Dissatisfaction is a great starting point, for it is right there that we have the most power, strength, and energy to push change through.

If you look at the word *hesitate*, you can find the word *sit*. Don't sit, but move. Hesitation stops energy. Move with the God-given momentum to make change happen. Start making the phone calls, asking people for referrals, calling the newspapers, and asking for help. Call on friends, call the library, and ask for references. Whatever the problem is, someone has handled the same dissatisfaction and sculpted it into an example of greatness.

The five steps for changing dissatisfaction are

1.   Identify what is bothering you.
2.   Figure out what would be the perfect outcome.
3.   Set a deadline for the change.
4.   Plan short-term steps. This is where most people go wrong in the day-to-day efforts. Plan your daily and weekly steps, plan your work, and work your plan.
5.   Most important, don't quit life. Persistence through the resistance is the key, and you will turn dissatisfaction into the force behind change.

12 Standing Around Gets You Nowhere.

Don't be afraid to ask for help or receive help. This advice was given to me by my father when I was in elementary school. I have always felt that I needed to prove to others and myself that I didn't need help. I remember one day my sixth grade class was going into another classroom to watch a movie. All the kids quickly found seats near their friends. I was too embarrassed to say that I couldn't find (see) a chair. When the teacher asked me if I wanted to sit, I said, "No, I'll be fine."

I was standing in the back corner of the room, leaning up against the wall. Ms. Fretas said, "David, are you sure you don't want to sit down? There are some seats in the front." I heard all the kids' voices laughing and talking in front of me. The thought of walking through the crowded classroom made me feel sick to my stomach and nervous. I didn't want to bump into anyone.

I said, "I'll be fine, really. I'll sit down in a minute." The lights went off, and the movie started. I was still standing in the back of the room, and I felt angry and out of place. I didn't know where my friends were sitting, and I couldn't find a seat. Questions and problems were running through my head: "Where are my friends sitting? I guess they don't want to sit near me. I wonder if they are my friends. Why don't they call me to sit with them? How long will I have to stand here before I find a seat? I hope no one is watching me and laughing. Why didn't I take Ms. Fretas' help?" I was a wreck.

I stood up for the entire film (about forty minutes). After the movie was over, Ms. Fretas asked me, "David, why didn't you sit down?"

I said, "I didn't feel like it."

She said, "If you couldn't find a chair, you should have asked. People don't mind helping when we ask nicely."

I remember feeling very uncomfortable, feeling like I didn't fit in, while standing up in the back of the classroom. I couldn't wait until the movie was over, but even when it was over, I was afraid that when the lights came on, people would laugh because they saw me standing there alone.

I have found that if we can be comfortable being uncomfortable, asking for what we need gets easier. Asking at first may feel a little uncomfortable, but if we can feel the feeling and do it anyway, asking gets comfortable. Don't do what I did and stand around feeling left out. Ask for and receive the help that you need to live, work, and play so that you can have, do, and become the person you desire to be.

13 No Attack— No Defense

This simple rule should be posted in every school, church, and company. I learned this at a very young age. It was January of 1978, and I was in the playground of number Ten School in Belleville, New Jersey. All the kids were playing: making a snowman, sliding down the hill, and having a snowball fight. It sounded as if everyone was having a really good time, and I desperately wanted to be involved.

So I picked up some snow and tossed it toward the crowd of kids playing. I bent down to pick up some more snow to make another snowball. As I stood up, I was hit in the face with a snowball. It was so cold that it was numbing. It felt like a rock. I was hit in the mouth, and blood started pouring out my lips and mouth. As I was walking to the door to go to the nurses office, I heard kids shouting, "Oh my goodness, he's a mess!"

My lip was swollen, and my gums were cut. My parents were called to come pick me up. My father came into the nurse's office and said, "Oh, he doesn't look too bad." During the car ride home, my father asked what had happened. I told him that everyone was having fun, and I just wanted to be involved.

That is when my father explained this rule: no attack—no defense. You don't have to attack people to be involved, and if you do attack someone, you will have to defend yourself. This simple rule has traveled with me in my personal and professional life. Attacks can come in many forms: rumors, notes, and other ways. When we invest our time in small talk (gossip), we can only accomplish small things, if anything.

Mother Teresa said, "If you judge someone, you'll have no time to love them." It's not too difficult to figure out what's wrong with someone else's life, personality, or situation. When we help people build on their strengths, face their fears, and become better people, we will be blessed and receive rewards unimaginable.

14 How to Build a Winner

I have been so blessed to be a part of many winning teams and organizations. I have had the pleasure of studying what makes a winner and what makes a loser. I believe the first step in any success—sports, work, a service group, whatever—is showing up. If you don't show up, nothing will happen. You will not get the workout, you will not meet the people, and you will not get the information you need to grow and excel.

The first winning team I was ever a part of was a bowling team. I was in the fifth grade, and the games were on Saturday mornings at ten. I couldn't really make out the individual pins; they looked like a white block at the end of the alley. I don't think I would have stuck it out the whole season if it hadn't been for my sister Michele. Michele is four years older than I am, and over the years she has helped me do many things.

I didn't know anyone on my bowling team, and the bowling alley was big, dark, and loud — hardly the perfect environment for a visually impaired child. When my mother picked me up after the third Saturday of bowling, I told her I was going to quit. She asked why, and I gave her some lame excuse. But she knew the truth. I really couldn't get around well, I didn't know anyone, and I was afraid. My mother told me the next week that my sister Michele would be coming with me. I sat up in my seat and said, "Really!"

"Not if you're going to quit," she said. I am not sure if Michele knew she would be going bowling, but if she didn't, she never let me know.

Every Saturday morning Michele would take me bowling. She even started keeping score and helping the other kids and parents. We kept individual and team scores, but it wasn't about winning or losing. We were having fun.

On the last Saturday of the season, I was both sad and excited. This week after the bowling, we would have lunch and an awards ceremony. I remember individual awards being handed out and wondering when we could leave. The final award was the Highest Pin Total for Teams. I was shocked to find out it was my team. I was so glad that my family had made me hang on until I caught on. I had made so many friends, learned to laugh at myself, and learned to hang in there even when I felt like quitting.

Twenty-some years later, the trophy is gone, the ribbons are lost, but the memories of winning still remain. None of this would have been possible unless my sister Michele was supportive and gave up her time to help build a champion.

Look for opportunities to help someone else, but don't give expecting something in return. Give knowing that if we give we receive.

Thank you, Michele.

15 Work Together or You'll Fall Apart.

This may sound like a ridiculous title for a chapter because everyone knows we must work together to achieve greatness. The question is why don't we do it. We all know what to do, but why don't we do it? I would like to examine this question and offer some ideas about how we could work together to make our lives happier, more satisfying, more prosperous, and even more productive.

I remember when I met Rich Ruffalo, a blind teacher at Belleville High School. He walked into study hall, introduced himself, and said, "David, I have heard a lot about you, and I'm going to help you."

"Help me do what?" I asked.

"Anything you want to do," he said. We began to talk informally, and he knew my older brother Vincent.

Rich invited me to my first weight-lifting contest three months later in December of 1983. I learned that nothing succeeds like success, and Rich offered to help train me. Who knew that this experience would change my life forever? I was only 105 pounds, and I squatted ninety pounds, benched pressed 130 pounds, dead lifted 145 pounds, and won the 114-weight class.

He would often invite me over to his house to work out in his gym. I lived only three or four blocks from Rich's house, so walking there was not a problem. For some reason I refused, giving excuse after excuse why I couldn't go to his house. He asked and asked, but each time I refused.

In June of 1984, the Association of Blind Athletes of New Jersey, a state chapter of the United States Association of Blind Athletes, was holding a national competition in St. Louis, Missouri. I was selected to the team, and after raising about eight hundred dollars, I was on my way to St. Louis.

I had a positive mental attitude but lacked coaching and weight-lifting technique. I bombed out of the contest, not making one of my first three lifts. I was extremely embarrassed. That day I watched Rich and many other well-trained athletes lift hundreds of pounds, totaling into the thousands of pounds. Rich encouraged me that day and continues to encourage me to this day.

Without coaching, all the positive mental attitude in the world cannot help you. A coach in hindsight can be an athlete's foresight. A coach will act as a road map and compass, providing information about roadblocks, detours, and shortcuts, if there are such things, on the road to success. I am so glad Rich continued to offer to train me, and in October of 1984, I started lifting weights with Rich and some of Rich's relatives and friends.

I learned about writing down goals and the importance of a weekly plan for obtaining them. I learned how humor can make a difficult problem easier. I learned how a positive mental attitude with proper technique can make up for brute strength. I learned that when you don't believe in yourself for whatever reason, a coach can see greatness and give you the resources to awaken the champion within so that you don't have worry and don't let a negative mental attitude or self-doubt destroy your dreams.

When I was in St. Louis, I witnessed a miracle happen in Rich's life as well. Rich was not only competing in weight lifting; he was also a champion javelin, discus, and shot-put thrower. I am not sure who came over to Rich and said, "Mr. Ruffalo, some kids from a school for the blind would like to meet you." These kids were all totally blind and had little, white canes, and Rich kneeled down to greet them. I remember these kids surrounding him, touching his arms and shoulders, and telling him that they were happy to meet him. Rich, with tears in his eyes, said he was so touched by these children that he was dedicating his life to helping others, and that is what he has done. I was glad to witness that miracle in his life and in the lives of those little kids that met my friend, mentor, and coach, Rich Ruffalo.

With all the good that comes out of working together, why do people refuse help when others are offering it? I think people are more interested in the hell they know than the heaven they don't. From my own experience, people hold onto the past if it's good, bad, or otherwise. We say, "It's fine. I'm getting by. I can handle it." Those are famous last words. I remember when I refused help. I was running in gym class and smacked a flagpole with my head. I woke up in the hospital, and my father explained that having help is not a sign of weakness. It's a sign that we want to remain strong.

What in your life needs changing? I know you don't have to think about what it is or take time to meditate or do some soul searching. I believe the problem we have is on the tip of our tongue, and we can articulate it immediately. We may be afraid to admit it, but it has been hiding in our closet, our garage, our office, and our car. Some people may even know about it. Whatever the problem we have in our life, someone has faced it and overcome it. So why not give it a try and improve your life? Let go of the past. Let go of the side of the pool so you can start swimming. Start taking on the challenges that you have. When we work together, we have power to take problems head on and make a huge difference in our life and in the lives of others around us.

Maybe you're saying, "Why should I let go of this problem? There is another one waiting around the corner." Or maybe you're saying, "Why should I let go of this one? I know I can handle this one." We make excuses for why we should or shouldn't do something, and holding onto a problem is a crutch. Holding onto the problem is just as bad as the problem.

Thinking that another problem is around the corner is a sign of negative thinking and will act as a self-fulfilling prophecy. You will create another problem around the corner so that you can point to the around-the-corner problem and say, "See, I told you." Focus your energy on greatness. Have a positive mental attitude about yourself, your family, your career, your health, and your entire life. Get a coach who has been there to make you realize that life is truly worth living. When we work together with like-minded people, miracles start to happen, walls get broken down, mountains become molehills, and dreams become realities.

Here are Rich's "Seven P's to Positively Enhance Performance" from the book of the same title:

1. Plummet enhances performance.
2. Pride enhances performance.
3. Passion enhances performance.
4. Purpose enhances performance.
5. People enhance performance.
6. Pressure enhances performance.
7. Prayer enhances performance.

16 The More You Learn the More You Earn.

I remember my uncle Frank Maulano saying to me sarcastically, "Oh, I forgot. When you're sixteen, you know everything." He went on to say, "The older I get the more I realize I don't know anything, and I'd better keep learning."

One of the most important things I've learned is not to be afraid to ask for help. When I went to college at East Stroudsburg University, I thought I knew everything: how to get along with different people, how to study, how to control myself. The first thing I learned is that I didn't know anything.

I recall that at our first freshmen dinner I was sitting by myself as people filed into the cafeteria. Out of the blue, an acquaintance from high school, Craig Burden, appeared and said, "Dave, I didn't know you were going to school here." He sat down, and the fun began.

We lived in the same dorm, Linden Hall, and Craig was a lifesaver. After dinner we talked and then went out for some cheese steaks to kill some time. The next morning Craig called me and asked me if I was going to breakfast. I said sure, and he met me in the front of the dorm. We walked down to the cafeteria. As we approached the cafeteria entrance, we talked about classes, girls, and probably girls in our classes.

I had no idea that there were two entrances in front of the cafeteria. One was a clear walk to the door, and the other one was a flight of five to six steps. I guess all the other times people directed me to the flat entrance, but today would be a new lesson that would grab my attention. As I walked and talked, I found myself in mid air with no ground under my feet. Thank God, I landed on the third step with Craig grabbing my arm and stopping me from falling backward. No scene was made, and I don't think anyone saw anything. But Craig said, "I guess you have a lot to learn around here."

He was right; I had a lot to learn then. I have a lot to learn now. We all have a lot to learn. One lesson that we must continue to relearn is not to be afraid to ask for help from people who are doing the things we want to do, going the places we want to go, and being the person we want to become.

Ask advice from the people who are doing what you want to do. I believe that success leaves clues. Don't be a defective detective. Go and collect the clues you need to become the person you wish to become. Go to the library, go to seminars, and ask questions of the people who are doing what you want to do.

We live in the information age; more information is available and accessible now than ever before. It is up to us to be collective detectives, not defective ones. Make phone calls, ask the librarian for help, ask your church leader, ask a good friend. We cannot stop learning, living, or loving.

I believe the qualities of our lives are determined by the people we meet, the books we read, and the questions we ask. Ask yourself, "What do I need to learn to get me from where I am now to where I want to go? What is stopping me from becoming the person I desire to become?" I believe examining ourselves and answering these questions will put us on the road to success.

17 Everyone Is in Sales.

I had the pleasure of speaking to a group of senior accountants at a conference. I asked them, "How many of you are in sales?" They didn't raise their hands. Even though I couldn't see them, I could tell they were uncomfortable, even squirming in their chairs. I then said, "Maybe I didn't make myself clear. Who in this room is in sales?" They started to get it, and one by one the hands started going up with confidence.

Everyone is in sales. We start when we are little babies, crying to have our dirty diaper changed or for a bottle because we are hungry. As we get older, we learn that hugs, smiles, and kisses are the currency for which people look. I believe that children are the best salespeople in the world, and we can learn all we need about sales from them.

As children grow up, they learn their ABCs. As adults, we must learn the ABCs of sales. They are not complicated; we just make them that way.

A—Attitude . . . about ourselves and the product or services we are selling
B—Belief . . . in ourselves and our product
C—Customer . . . know what our customers need or want

That works in school, at home, and at work. We must have a positive attitude, we must believe in what we are doing, and we must think about other people as our customers. Life is a two-way street, not just a one-way street. We must think about other people and about how they will benefit from what we are offering. Husbands must think of their wives, children must think of their parents, teachers must think of their students, and employees must think of their companies.

Remember that famous radio station W.I.I.F.M. "What's in it for me?" We must think about what's in it for them. A win-win situation is when you and I both win; this is the basis for progress. Bruce Springstein says, "No one wins unless everyone wins." Figure out how everyone can win. Then we'll be surrounded by lots of winners.

18 Kids Have Other Ideas.

Kids sometimes have a problem listening but never a problem copying. I never realized how true this statement was until Mariann and I had our son, David Junior. During dinner one evening, David started to fuss and cry. After a day of working, sometimes my patience is short. I said, "Come on, David, please just eat."

Mariann said, "Dave, he just wants to roll his sleeves up like his daddy." Mariann has the ability to quickly take the steam out of the internal pressure cooker; this is a wonderful skill we all should work on. We need to help people stay cool, not be the kind of person who stirs the pot and gets people hot.

We live in the age of fast computers and fast cars, so we get frustrated when things don't go our way right away. We need to learn from children and be childlike. Notice I said childlike, not childish.

It was a beautiful afternoon in sunny southern California. It was a Little League championship baseball game. As with any championship game, the field was packed with friends, family members, and other interested individuals. It was a tie game, and the score was two to two in the bottom of the seventh inning. The bases were loaded, the count on the batter was three balls and two strikes, and the pitcher was just about to throw the ball. You could cut the tension with a knife. With the next pitch, one team would be a winner, and one would go home defeated.

The pitcher called the catcher out to the pitcher's mound. The pitcher was pointing at the ground, so the first and third basemen jogged over to see what they were looking at. Then the umpires called time-out, and the outfielders came to see what was going on. Then the three base runners walked to the pitcher's mound to see what was going on. The catcher ran to the bench to get a box. Evidently, there was a lizard on the field, and they wanted to help it. The crowd was shocked. The catcher said, "I know this is an important game, but we don't want to see the lizard get hurt." After the lizard was removed from the field, the game resumed. But everyone in that Little League game learned an important lesson: Games are important, but helping others is more important.

Never be too busy or involved in something to offer someone a helping hand. It may be the same hand that helps you one day.

19 Everyone Needs a Hug.

I love hugs. Maybe it is because I come from a large Italian family. Maybe it's because I've always been involved with teams. Maybe it just feels good. I believe a hug can change the world. Maybe not the whole world, but a hug can change the world of a family member or friend.

I like the acronym H.U.G. The letters stand for Helping Unlock Greatness. Hugs feel good when you're happy, when you're sad, when you're mad at your boss, when you've been promoted, when you're sweaty and dirty after a race, when you need courage to enter the race. Hugs feel great. They're the best battery chargers in the world. Hugs liberate the soul, release the tension, and free the worries.

Hugs do not always have to be physical; they can be emotional. An emotional hug can be a thinking-of-you letter, a thank-you card, or a phone call. I have tried to make a habit of calling people when I think of them. Many times they will say, "Yes, I was thinking of you as well." Hugs make a great deposit in the emotional fuel tank.

Spiritual hugs are wonderful as well. I love sitting in the warm sun on the beach or in the mountains near a powerful waterfall. I am just glad I'm alive, and I thank God for the opportunity to breathe the fresh air and feel the warm sun. You don't have to get back to nature to pray and receive spiritual hugs. I have enjoyed spiritual hugs on the train while I was just relaxing and giving thanks for my wonderful family, friends, and experiences.

If you have never felt a spiritual hug, then you should make some time to experience twenty minutes of peace, which would be equivalent to a ten-day vacation. H.U.G is also an acronym for Help Unlock God's will for our lives.

We often attribute it to human nature when people take shortcuts or try to cut corners, but there is no corner cutting when praying. You're either praying or you're not. You can't be praying and also thinking,

"Hm, I hope we get that shipment today." When we pray, we relax, reflect, and renew our commitments to God. The peace that comes from consulting with God and receiving His divine wisdom is a powerful hug.

I remember receiving a great spiritual hug when I was fifteen. I was home from school, and my father was home from the hospital, recovering from cancer surgery. My father complained of shoulder and upper-arm pain for a few days. I hated knowing that my father was sick and that there was nothing I could do about it. My family raised me to ask, pray, and believe for miracles, and that is what I started doing.

I was lying on the couch in our family room, just relaxing, and praying for relief of the pain in my dad's arm. A huge screen appeared before me with an extremely bright light. I saw my father lying in a blue shirt on a table. His arm and shoulder were in the same bright light as the background. The next morning I asked my father how he felt, and he said fine. I asked him about his arm, and he said it felt great. Then he asked me how I knew his arm was feeling better. I began to tell him the story about the blue shirt and the bright light on his arm. My father began to cry. He said we both shared in a miracle. I think that was one of the greatest hugs I ever received.

Don't be afraid to give or receive a hug. It just may be the thing that will help you unlock greatness. Hug a friend with a thinking-of-you card. Send a thinking-of-you email or a thank-you note to someone who did something nice for you days, weeks, even years ago. Share a hug with a friend, family member, or someone else who needs one.

It is hard to give a hug without receiving one in return.

20 What Are You Doing to Other People?

I had the pleasure of speaking at The Verona, New Jersey's Unico club, which is an Italian American organization. After the meeting, a gentlemen, one of the members, came up to me, grabbed my cheek, and said, "Son, there are lifters in this world, and then there are leaners. You, my friend, are a lifter. You really lifted my spirit today."

It is amazing to me that by sharing our heartbreaks, worries, and feelings with other people, they are liberated. I have found that most people have been conditioned to hide their feelings. When people live by the rule of "Don't let your guard down," I generally find that these people become bitter and are usually stuck in a miserable situation, job, or relationship. The idea "If my feelings are callous, then I will not get hurt" only stifles our thoughts and does not allow us to really get to know others or them to have the opportunity to know us.

It is easy for us to show our emotions to others when everything is going well and to hide our dark feelings when everything is a big, sloppy mess.

I believe that when things are a mess, we need others to know what we are thinking, feeling, or doing. We must share our feelings with people who will not reprimand us for our thoughts. We need to share these feelings with someone who will encourage us to move forward. We need coaches, friends, and counselors who will provide us with the positive feedback and resources we need, people who will not leave our emotional tanks empty by filling them up with discouragement.

The comment that the gentlemen made to me about lifters and leaners really stuck with me. I believe we must surround ourselves with friends, teachers, and coaches who will lift our spirits when we are down and with good friends who we can lean on when the whole world walks out.

We must spend our time building bridges to the world and not walls blocking and locking ourselves from the world.

Part IV
Associating

21 Two Heads Are Better Than One.

When I first read about the mastermind principle, I realized that this activity more than all other activities is the most determining factor of all success laws, rules, or principles. When we work together, think together, and dream together, we bring into power a heavenly perspective of harmony. When we are under the influence of harmony, we have the ability to draw out confidence, resources, and creativity that are jam-packed with the universe of potential.

A mastermind group can be composed of at least two but no more than eight individuals. The group can meet in person or over the phone. Groups should meet weekly for optimum performance. A mastermind group is like putting two candles together. When two candles are alone, their flames will only grow so big; however, put the two flames together, and you'll see the flames immediately more than double in size.

Everyone in the group must be comfortable with each other. There can be no egos in this group. E.G.O. stands for Earthly Guide Only or Edging God Out. The ego is a little thing that can destroy many big or potentially big things.

I have been offered help in my life, but because my ego was running the show, I refused the help and in turn refused a lifetime of experience and know-how. I was offered weight-lifting training from my friend Rich Ruffalo, but it took a defeat to remove my ego and make me realize I needed his assistance.

Mark Riesenberg offered his services many times, but again I refused his generous offers. When we have the courage to ask for help, then miracles happen. I must say I don't believe in miracles—I rely on them. You may be reading or listening to this and saying, "I don't need help. I've gotten here on my own." The first sign that you need help is thinking or feeling you don't need any help at all. Don't be afraid to ask for help. If people tell you they are self-made millionaires, that just proves that ingrates can make money.

The mastermind group should meet for one hour. Let me tell you that it is the most liberating hour of your week. No one can or should feel the need to criticize another member. No one can be uninspiring, and the meeting should end with everyone feeling like a winner.

I remember sitting with my coach Rich Ruffalo in his house in Belleville, New Jersey, in 1986. He told me to make a mental note that we were going to be motivational speakers, and one day we would speak to companies, schools, and organizations to share with them how we overcame our blindness. It still amazes me that something he said to me more than fifteen years ago is making all my family's dreams come true.

You see, you don't have to have a formal mastermind group, but I encourage you to put one together. I hope that as you're reading this, names are coming to mind of people you would consider having in your group. I hope you are jotting down their names, not letting them be fleeting thoughts but leaping thoughts in your mind.

Design your own personal board of directors that will steer your life personally and professionally. I believe we need more than a physical coach but also a mental coach with books we should read and tapes we should listen to. We need a spiritual coach who will keep us in tune with the greater power in our universe whom I call God. You see, if we are not on track spiritually, our faith will dwindle like a fire on a late, cold night. We must also have an emotional coach who allows us to stay in tune with our relationships. We need someone who has the ability to make and maintain friends, someone who will encourage building relationships because, as you already know, the quality of our lives is determined by the books we read and the people we meet.

22 Look and Listen for Love.

Have you heard the story about the man who wanted to move up the hill? One day a young man decided he wanted to move up the hill to where the houses are bigger, the air is cleaner, and life is better, or so he thought. He started walking up the long, winding hill. He came across a man watering his flowers and asked, "Excuse me, sir, are there any houses for sale?"

The man replied, "Yes, there is a house up the hill for sale." The man then put his watering can down and asked, "Where are you from?

"Just down the hill."

"Why are you looking to move?"

"Oh," the man quickly replied, "down the hill people are mean and very negative, and some are thieves."

The man watering his flowers picked up his watering can and said, "You'll find them up here also."

I didn't know when I met Mariann that I had met one of the most wonderful people in the world. My mother told me that you don't really know people until you spend a lot of time with them. The more time I spent with Mariann, the more I liked her.

In May of 1996, I went to the doctor for an eye exam. The doctor said, "David, I think if we remove a cataract in your right eye, you may be able to see better. I would like you to meet with another specialist for a second opinion." I visited the specialist, and he agreed that cataract surgery might improve my sight in my right eye. Mariann and I went back to the first doctor with the specialist's report. After some discussion, we agreed to the surgery and scheduled an operating date.

Mariann and I were doing some insurance paperwork in the waiting room when the doctor entered the room. He said to Mariann, "You're not planning to have any children with him are you?" I was blown away.

Mariann said, "Yes."

The doctor said, "I wouldn't if I were you." Then he put his hand on my shoulder and said, "David, your child could have what you have, and you know how difficult your life is. You wouldn't want to bring someone into this world who has what you have, would you?" I couldn't speak because I was too busy fighting back the tears. He then said, "You two had better think about it."

Mariann and I were silent; we didn't speak in the office. We didn't talk while we waited for the elevator; we didn't speak on the elevator even though we were alone. I had no idea what Mariann was thinking. I was still holding back the tears and wondering what would happen. *Will Mariann leave me?* The feelings of worry, stress, tension, anger, and fear were pumping through my veins, pulling at my back and neck. Millions of thoughts and images raced through my head.

The elevator door eventually opened, and we were walking toward the exit. Mariann grabbed my arm and said, "David, we're not going to listen to those doctors. We're going to have a family. Everything will be fine, and if there is a problem, you'll be the best role model in the world."

I wish I could have bottled that *wow* emotion. It was love, support, joy, peace, and happiness all rolled up into one Mariann.

Surround yourself with people who can see the possibilities for you. Encourage others and see the possibilities for them as well. As you know, life is an echo; we get what we give. There are two ways to build the tallest building in town. You can tear down everyone else's building, or you can build a strong foundation and use great support. With respect, time, love, and care, we can build the strongest families, churches, schools, groups, and organizations. Support others and remain strong.

23 The Best Advice I Can Give

A high school student asked me during a presentation, "What is the best advice you can give a high school student?" After thinking about this question for a few minutes, this was my reply: "Don't let people discourage you from living your dreams."

Many people will tell you, "Oh, that's a good idea, but . . ." Anything that comes after the "but" is a list of reasons why you shouldn't take action on your idea, thoughts, or even your dreams. The other day I shared some good news with someone, and the person replied, "David, I hate to burst your bubble, but that's not the way the industry works."

Please do not confuse the comments I'm talking about with advice from people in your mastermind group or on your personal board of directors. I am saying be careful of sharing your goals and dreams with people who are not like-minded. Only share your dreams with people who will see things for you. Only share your dreams with people who have better long-term vision than you have. Share your dreams with people who will help you make them happen.

Have you heard the analogy of the crab in the pot on the stove? If there is one crab in a pot on the stove, the crab will jump, scratch, pull, and claw its way out of the pot. If there are two or more crabs in the pot, one crab will try to get out, but the other crabs will be on its back, pulling it down. It's as if the other crabs are saying, "Hey, where are you going? You're not leaving without me." This is a perfect analogy because some people do not want to see you succeed; your success causes them to feel inferior.

We must share our dreams with people who will see us working toward and accomplishing our goals. Be encouraged by people who say, "How about trying it this way?" As for the people who say, "That's a good idea but . . . ," we must remind them to get off their "buts" and to concentrate on all the things they can do.

There is a story about a woman who walked into a seafood restaurant and asked, "Do you serve crabs? The manager quickly replied, "Miss, we serve anyone!"

The best advice I can give to you is be true to yourself and live your dreams. Don't let any crabs hold you back. Get out there and make it happen.

24 Surrounding Ourselves with Greatness

When I was growing up, I remember my mother saying, "Your friends are like elevators; they will bring you up or down—the choice is yours." I didn't really listen to her. I thought, "Yeah, whatever." But the more I grow up, the more I realize how right she was. Our friends are like elevators, and they bring up and down our

- Energy level
- Self-esteem
- Confidence
- Aspirations
- Adventure
- Will to succeed
- Hope
- Prayers
- Will to achieve
- Lifestyle

When our energy level is up and our minds are open to possibilities, greatness just happens. If we surround ourselves with people who deflate our energy level, we lose ambition and even the will to achieve. We tend to compare ourselves with people who are doing less than we are, which gives us a false sense of security, a false sense of well being and well doing. We must surround ourselves with a pace car, someone who will encourage us, inspire us, and even empower us to greatness.

My coach, mentor, and friend Rich Ruffalo is someone who has served and is still serving as my mentor — a pace car. I sometimes refer to Rich as a gardener, sprinkling seeds of ideas around and nourishing them with encouragement and enthusiasm. More important, he nourishes me with his courageous actions. Another person who has acted as a mentor, coach, and pace car is my good friend Mark Riesenberg. Mark's license plate says "BALANCE," and I believe he exemplifies balance personally and professionally.

Mark encouraged me to write this book. We were sitting in a small pizza parlor in West Orange, New Jersey, and he said, "David, the book is already written. All you have to do is have the discipline to put it on paper." He was right. Mark has the ability to give a simple formula for success. He doesn't waste time by going through all the pros and cons, which muffle dreams. I first met Mark when he was serving as a consultant for the First Occupational Center of New Jersey. He was helping me with some sales skills, and we have never stopped talking. Mark introduced me to personal development tapes. He first loaned me a Ken Blanchered tape series, then a Brian Tracy, and then a Steven Covy. I've been hooked ever since. I now make it part of my daily routine to listen to tapes I receive from family and friends or borrow from the library or the bookstore. I seek out what makes some people successful and others not so successful.

Mark's sound advice has assisted me with personal relationships, reminding me that there are no quick fixes and that we must not just *go* through a problem but *grow* through a problem.

I remember Mark asking me what one of my personal goals was. I was quick to say, "To have a house in the Pocono Mountains."

"Why?" he asked.

"So when I have a bad day at work, Mariann and I can take a trip up there to relax and spend time with each other."

"David," he quickly replied, "you've got it all wrong. A master motivator has the ability to enroll someone into a vision, to help someone achieve greatness. Picture this in your mind's eye. You just made a huge sale: twenty thousand books and ten thousand tapes, with an ongoing two-year contract. You worked so hard for it, and you were up against so many other quality speakers; yet you're the one with the contract. You feel so good, and now you Mariann and the family are going to your mountain resort to plan, relax, and celebrate."

Mark explained that our mind goes to work on whatever we think about, so we might as well focus on greatness. Mark also taught me about the three things that stop people more than anything else does from achieving their goals: criticizing, complaining, and blaming. These are the three horsemen of failure. If I ever call Mark with a problem, twenty seconds into the conversation he asks, "David, you're not complaining, are you? David, I am not about complaining; I'm about solutions." Mark told me that the problem can be stated in seventeen words or less, and then we must spend the rest of our time focusing on the solution.

When we surround ourselves with people who focus on possibilities, not problems, the load seems lighter. Mark and Rich are two people who are not afraid of working and taking action. Their coaching and pushing have given me the courage to move forward when fear, logic, and doubt would tell me not to. If someone or something is stopping you, then stop it! Don't spend time with people who are going to bring you down, but surround yourself with people who will psych you up!

25 Getting Along with Others

The most useful skill in the world is the ability to get along with others. If we can't get along with people, whatever we are trying to accomplish will be difficult. If it's at school, at work, at church, or wherever, we must be able to get along with and communicate with others. I have found that before any business deal is made, we must *friend raise* before we can *fund raise*.

The first step toward developing solid relationships is a firm handshake. I find nothing more aggravating than receiving a handshake like an old, dead fish. A handshake must convey confidence. It should not cause a fracture in the hand, but it should let the other person know that you are not afraid, that you feel great, that you are confident.

Remember the commercial that says, "You only get one chance to make a first impression." If someone greets me with a weak handshake, I know something isn't right. When I receive a firm handshake, I feel the message of confidence. As you are shaking someone's hand, say, "It's a pleasure to meet you."

We must develop rapport with other people. People like to work with people to whom they can relate. We must find common ground to stand on. Use the information at hand to stimulate conversation. For example, look at the pictures, plaques, or certificates in someone's office and remark, "Oh, I see you're a member of the Lion's Club. How long have you been a member?" People love talking about themselves. Find the hot topic that gets them talking, and then you'll be on the road to developing a relationship.

Nothing is sweeter to people's ears than their own name. Call people by their name. Ask the question, "May I call you Robert, or do you prefer Bob?" Don't assume anything. Ask. I have been in meetings where people lost sales or contracts because they were not paying attention to detail. They forgot someone's name. They called the person Sue instead of Susan, for example.

Stay away from controversial conversations. My uncle Joe Maulano told me to never talk about the deadly three: personal relationships, religion, or money. These are areas that are very personal, and people are very passionate about these topics. Stay away from these topics when first meeting or working with someone. These topics can quickly turn a discussion into a heated debate.

Put people at ease. Some people lighten a room when they walk in it, and others lighten a room when they leave it. We must make people feel comfortable first with us then with themselves. Conversations about vacations, children, or special events lighten people's hearts. There is an old saying: "The way to people's hearts is through their stomachs." I believe the way to people's hearts is through their interests. If someone likes to talk about baking, talk about recipes. If they like to talk about restaurants, talk about restaurants. I have learned that everyone has something to offer; we just have to figure out what that something is.

Stay in touch with people! Don't just meet people and leave their business card in your jacket pocket, only to throw it out weeks later. Enter their contact information in your computer database or your Rolodex. Stay in contact with follow-up notes, phone calls, postcards, annual reports, lunch meetings, FYI letters, and holiday greetings. If you happen to see them or their company on TV or in a newspaper, send a note of congratulations.

We cannot be successful on our own. We need the help, support, and encouragement of those around us. When we take a few minutes to stay in touch with important people, they will take the time to stay in touch with us. Send notes, pictures, or thinking-of-you cards. I have found that a little correspondence can generate calls from people who say, "I was having a horrible day, and your note made my day." Be the person who goes above and beyond the call of duty. Keep your family, friends, and community together. Keep the channels of verbal and written communication open. As the song says, you will find out that "it's a small world after all."

Part V
Dreaming
&
Becoming

26 Hang on Until You Catch on.

What are you hanging onto? What thoughts, ideas, or addictions are you holding onto from last week, last month, maybe even last year? If we hold onto things that hold us back, we will never have the time or opportunity to move forward.

There was a small, single-engine plane flying some military brass and their family members home for the Christmas holiday. The plane started experiencing some problems. The motor started to mutter and putter, and the plane began to dip and dive. Everyone on the small plane was concerned. After a few minutes, the pilot got the plane under control and said, "We need to lighten the plane's load. Please cooperate."

Everyone started to nervously look around. What would be thrown out? People said, "You can't throw out my luggage. It holds all my clothes, all my belongings. That's my life in there." The captain heard the complaints and made this announcement: "Your bags, personal belongings, and luggage can stay; however, that means you must go!" The pilot then asked for some volunteers "who would like to leave first."

I am sure that most, if not all, of the individuals watched with horror as their bags, luggage, and suitcases fell to the water. I am sure this beat the plane's falling into the ocean or into the side of a mountain.

What are the things you are holding onto that are preventing you from grasping the future? Someone once said that you'll never steal second if your foot is firmly planted on first. You'll never learn to swim if you hold onto the side of the pool.

We must have the courage to let go of the past if we are going to grasp the future. You can't give or receive anything with a closed fist. So open up your hand, open up your mind, and open up your heart. Let the new possibilities come in, and let the negative anchors of the past sink to the bottom of the sea. Let go. Now, let's go!

27 Making Deposits Count

We must make deposits if our dreams are to become a reality. If our dreams are going to come true, then we must help others make their dreams become a reality. When we sit down with people and find out what they would like to accomplish, we allow our creative juices to go to work. If we hide our creative juices and use them only for our own benefit, we neglect others and, in turn, neglect ourselves.

We must make deposits into the emotional bank accounts of others. An idea is a deposit, and an insult is a withdrawal.

When I was in fourth grade, my mother started working in a bank as a teller. I asked her what she did, and she told me she helped the bank customers manage their money. Some would come to make deposits, and some would come to make withdrawals. Our emotions work the same way. When we receive a complement, a deposit is made into our emotional bank account. When someone makes a derogatory comment, a withdrawal is taken from this account.

I remember being in my parents' car one time and hearing my parents discussing my blindness. My father said, "Joan, David is going to be fine. We are going to give him the proper information and inspiration so that he can lead a normal life." This was one of the greatest deposits I have ever received. I think of this as the core deposit. When we find out that someone believes in us, it is powerful. Notice the word *we* in the word *power*. We are in power.

Are you making deposits on your dreams? Are you asking yourself the questions that are going to drive you forward, or are you asking yourself the questions that are going to hold you back? We also have the ability to make deposits and withdrawals on our own emotional bank accounts. If we sit around wishing, hoping, dreaming, and not acting on our dreams, one day we will wake up very discouraged because we are not where we want to be. Reading books, listening to tapes, and surrounding ourselves with supportive people will make deposits in our account.

If we hang around people who see only the problems, the worries, and the confusion, huge withdrawals will be taken from our account. If there are three people in a room and two are negative, then you can bet all three people will develop a negative slant on whatever the group is discussing. We must not let people dump their emotional garbage on the floor of our lives.

Ask yourself this question: "Will this activity make a deposit or withdrawal from my emotional bank account?"

The law of giving applies to emotional bank accounts. The more you give complements, the more they will be given to you. People who bring misery wherever they go and always make withdrawals from others' accounts will have withdrawals taken from their own accounts. We must monitor deposits and withdrawals to make sure that the people around us are receiving the proper investments they need to become rich on the inside.

28 Keep Your Ear on the Ball.

My fourth grade teacher, Ms. Petrillo, in School Ten in Belleville, New Jersey, gave this advice to me. She said that this was the best piece of advice she could give to teachers, educators, and students: Make it okay for all students to fit in. This sure can be a tall order, but it is life-changing for all involved. For the students who do not have impairments, making accommodations teaches creativity. For the students who need the accommodations, it allows them the opportunity to play and learn on a level playing field.

When I was in fourth grade, we played base-ball, football, and tennis, and we had school Olympics during gym class. My teacher, Ms. Petrillo, and the gym teacher, Ms. Meola, made it possible for me to be involved. One memory that sticks out is playing soft-ball in the school yard. Ms. Petrillo was the pitcher, and when it was my turn at the plate, she made sure all the students were quiet. She would tell me to keep my ear on the ball, and then she would bounce the softball to the plate. I was able to listen to the bounc-ing ball and usually hit it on the third bounce.

I don't think there was anything more satisfy-ing than my being able to hit the ball into the outfield. I felt like everyone else. Ms. Petrillo would have one of my classmates stand at first base and call me, so I knew where to run. I do not think anyone really cared that there was a special accommodation; the game wasn't changing, the rules were the same, and every-one was playing.

Everyone has strengths and weaknesses, and it is important to show people that they can be involved, regardless of who they are or what physical limita-tions they have. Some students are better at spelling, some are better in gym class, and some are better in the school plays. No matter who you are, you have strengths.

My advice for you is to keep your eye on the ball. If you, like me, can't see the ball, keep your ear on the ball. If you can't keep your eye or ear on the ball, find a different ball that you enjoy and keep your eye and ear on it. Figure out what you like to do, find someone who has similar interests, and figure out how that person did what you want to do.

You see, success leaves clues, and we need to pick up those clues and put the pieces together for our own life. One day someone is going to come to *you* and ask how *you* did it. Because you were creative, because you persevered, because you persisted through the resistance, you will be able to hold your chin up and help someone else overcome.

29 The Best Nation in the World

The best nation in the world is our imagi*nation*. Our imagination is the workshop of our mind. This is the place where dreams are born, ideas are nourished, and plans are made. This is a safe place where we can put things together and also take things apart. This is the place where poor become rich, problems are solved, and battles are won.

I have found that the imagination does not work to its full potential when we are lying on the couch doing nothing, but when we are with like-minded people. Our imagination is triggered by the laughter we share when we are with the people we love. Our imagination juices begin flowing when our barriers are down and we are allowed to be ourselves.

I believe we build walls around our imagination because we are afraid of others laughing at us. We are afraid to allow our imagination to take over because we are afraid of our ideas, afraid of the solutions we find to our problems, and afraid of the person we might become. We put our imagination on the shelf and tell ourselves we must be practical, realistic, and even serious.

I have often been accused of not being serious enough. There is nothing wrong with being serious, but we must also make room for our imagination. We must have the ability to say "Why not?" or "I can do that" or (most powerful) "I am not afraid of the work, so let's get to it" when our imagination juices start flowing. Our imagination allows us to take another look at our lives from a different perspective. It allows us to play and replay different scenarios in our mind. Imagination is not just for children but also for us practical, realistic, hardworking adults.

We must use our imagination to help us create, not destroy. If we do not take control of our imagination, it is like an unharnessed horse bucking, kicking, and wildly running out of control, headed nowhere. When our imagination is focused on a definite purpose like an artist with a blank piece of paper and a full paint set, we start to create. A stroke here and an outline there, a background and now a dream—like those of a master artist, the picture becomes clearer and clearer until it becomes alive, leaping off the page for all to see and admire.

I have been asked the question, "How do you know the difference between a thought, an idea, and a dream dropped into our minds from heaven?" The only way I can explain the answer is through a personal experience.

When I was in twelfth grade, I had a class that inspired my life. The class was Mass Communications at Belleville High School in Belleville, New Jersey. In this class, we had our own TV and radio station. One day while broadcasting on TV, my dream began to come alive, and it never left. I opened my mouth, and the words just flowed. I loved being on TV and on the radio. When I was on the air, I enjoyed encouraging others, and that was the start of my dream. It was the first splash of paint on my imagination's canvas. The class instructor, Mrs. McCabe, told me I had a gift and had better not let it go, but I should, as with all great gifts, give it away for all to see and appreciate. I always enjoyed encouraging others, but now I was being encouraged to encourage others. It felt right.

Many times we will be approached and asked to get involved in others' dreams, but it won't feel right. The way we can tell the difference between an idea, a thought, and a dream is that a dream feels right; it fits like a glove.

A thought can be like a cloud just floating by, but a dream sticks to our minds like Velcro and becomes a part of us. That is a dream, and we must nourish that dream with the proper sunshine and rain to allow it to grow. We must also fertilize our dreams with rejections, so we can learn and understand what works and what doesn't. An idea gets us interested, but a dream gets us excited.

I truly believe our dreams are inside us, and it is our job to bring them out. Get to work. The dream is closer than you think!

30 If at First You Succeed, Try Something Harder.

We have all read or heard this famous quote: "If at first you don't succeed, try, try again." This is the first motivational quote I ever heard. My mother shared it with me. Years later she shared another quote with me: "If at first you succeed, try, try something harder." I have found this quote to be true first in weight lifting and now in business. Someone also shared with me this quote: "If at first you don't succeed, deny ever trying."

I have found through years of extensive research that many people try something, achieve whatever they tried, and then stop. I believe this is just as bad as not succeeding and giving up. Sometimes we succeed on the first try, and then we get busy basking in the glory of our own little accomplishments. This is not a winning attitude.

Succeeding and not succeeding are the two reasons we need goals. When we don't succeed, we need goals to keep us focused. I once heard someone say that success is not hocus pocus but focus focus. When we don't succeed at something, the easy thing is to say, "That's it. I give up." This is also not a winning attitude.

Ask yourself these questions:

1. What do I want from life? Many people demand nothing from life and nothing from themselves. When you demand nothing, you get nothing.

2. What do I need to learn to become the person I desire to be?

We must take the time to answer these tough questions. Sometimes we see the questions but do not take the time to answer them. I have been told they are too difficult to answer. However, I am confident that if we take the time to answer these questions, we can eliminate stress, worry, and confusion in our personal and professional lives.

One day in college I tried to tell a professor I couldn't do something because I was blind. It was an excuse because I wanted to get out of some work. He said, "David, listen to me. Life is tough. Now what? You can do this. Go figure it out." He was right. Life can be tough. When we ask ourselves tough questions and take the time to give realistic answers, we will find that we can succeed. We will also find that when we do things we didn't know we could, other things get easier.

Train yourself to try difficult things. You will find that you will not be afraid to be a trailblazer, a leader, and the captain of your own ship and your own soul.

31 A Secret Everyone Should Be Told

Everyone loves hearing a secret, and maybe even more so, most people love telling one. I know a secret that has helped me, and I think everyone should be told it. A secret to living a happy life is not just having what you want but, more important, wanting what you have. That's the secret that changes the focus from our outside to our inside.

We all have spent time figuring out what community we would love to live in, the best car we can drive, and the woman or man we would love to spend some time with. But how much time do we spend appreciating the things we have before us? Have you ever spent minutes, days, even years dreaming of what you want out of life but then woke up, realizing that your friends, co-workers, and family members were awake working on their dreams?

That is a tough pill to swallow. We must break down the barriers of laziness, jealousy, and envy and work on ourselves. Have you ever watched your brother, friend, or co-worker achieve something great, get into the school, get the job, buy the house, or get the date? Then your internal pressure cooker starts to launch jealousy, anger, or disgust throughout your body, spirit, and mind.

This internal activity is just another distraction preventing us from becoming the person we desire to become. The secret to life is to love who you are—warts and all. You see, if you have a pulse, you have a problem. Don't just say, "Well, I have these problems, and that is why I am down here. They have all the luck, resources, and money, and they are up there." We must continue to focus our energy on our strengths and not on what we don't have.

I remember when I was in tenth grade. I received a call from an acquaintance who was also blind. I am not sure what the person's motivation for calling me was, but this is what the person said: "David, a lot of your friends are going to be dating now, but since you are blind and will not be able to drive, dating will be difficult if not impossible." The caller went on to explain, "I am telling you this for your own good. I just wanted to explain this to you because this was my experience." Then came the explanation.

I do not know how long I let this fear hold me back. The worry I felt was too heavy for me to carry. I tried and tried to put this thought out of my head, but the harder I tried, the more it showed up. The more I thought about it, the more examples of what they said became real. One day I received some advice from one of my teachers, Mrs. Russo, that helped me. She told me, "David don't try so hard. Just be friends with people, and everything will fall into place."

I had to learn to like me before anyone else would. How can anyone like you if you don't even like yourself? That is why we must change the focus from the outside to the inside. The clothes we wear and the style of our hair are on the outside. When we change things on the inside, we change how we feel about ourselves and then how we feel about others.

When you want what you have—yourself— then everything will start to fall into place. Enjoy yourself, love yourself, and tell yourself three, four, or five times a day, "I love myself. I like myself." After doing that a couple times, you can't help but smile.

Slow down. Enjoy what's around you, and use all your senses. Appreciate the white, puffy clouds in the sky; some people can't see them. Appreciate the sounds of the birds singing; some people can't hear them. Appreciate the sweet fragrance of a rain shower or a blooming flower; some people can't smell them. Appreciate the food you eat; some people don't have it or cannot taste it. I believe that gratitude can change our attitude.

At our wedding, the best man, John Apicella, said, "To David and Mariann, may you live as long as you want but never want as long as you live." That is my wish for you.

32 Just Turn It On.

I believe we can turn our emotions on when we need to. We can also decide to turn our mind over to possibilities. When our mind is in a *practical* state, just dealing with the information at hand, problems seem insurmountable, worries seem powerful, and life seems difficult. When we turn our mind to possibilities, the load seems lifted.

Two things drive us: pleasure and pain. Pleasure is the hope of something great: a victory, a vacation, good health, and the future. We are also driven by pain.

My Aunt Rose smoked for fifty-five years and had a stroke. Even in the hospital, she was smoking. The doctor explained that if she didn't stop smoking she would die. I know she loved smoking, but she also loved living. She told me quitting was hard, but it was worth it. She said, "David, I loved having a cigarette at the beach, after dinner, while reading the newspaper, when having coffee, or whenever. It was painful, but I wanted to live."

What do you love to do? We must identify this because it is a driving force. We must make sure that *it* is driving us closer to family and dreams, not farther away. If it is an encouraging, helpful, community-enhancing idea that no one will be hurt by, then it is probably a positive force. However, if the force is one of deception and confusion, it very well may be a negative force, even a farce.

When trying to determine the difference between a negative and positive force, ask yourself, "How will I feel when my mother and grandmother read about this in the front page of the newspaper? How will they feel when they find out? Will they be proud or disappointed? Will they say I always was a good kid, or will they say I was always a bad egg?

Will they say I was always looking to make a quick buck?"

You may be reading this and saying this is negative talk. Yes, it is, but this is a way that we can use pain as a motivator. We must be aware of the motives behind our own motivation. We must not simply let emotion drive us. We are sophisticated individuals, not wild animals. We have the ability to make decisions, analyze, and plan. Wild animals work on instinct and reaction. When we have a purpose in mind, the image becomes clear, the plan is designed, and the mission is more than half accomplished.

We can tap into a bigger power that will give us the will to keep on keeping on. Turn the key, take off the mental brakes, and step on the accelerator. Your dreams are waiting for you!

33 Getting from the Sidelines into the Ball Game

Are you on the sidelines, watching the world go by? It is so amazing how our mind affects everything we do. When we are on the mental sidelines, our body feels stuck, like we have the brakes on. You can feel it in your gut, in your legs, even in your heart. The best way to get off the sidelines is to get off the sidelines. That may sound simplistic or maybe even stupid, but it's true. Taking action on our dreams and putting motion behind our ideas can get us off the sidelines.

Picture yourself sitting on a diving board, ready to jump into a refreshing pool on a steamy, hot day. You want to jump in. You bounce a bit, and then you tell yourself, "Just do it." The next thing you know—splash, boom, wow—you're in the water. You're moving your arms and legs, and it feels great. You tell everyone around you, "It's not that bad. It actually feels great." You wonder why you were ever hesitant to jump. You wonder why you had the brakes on.

We may have thought something was hard because a friend, a teammate, a co-worker, someone told us it was hard. The person may not have been lying; for the person it really may have been hard. But do not let other people make determinations for you. Experience things for yourself.

We will never learn to swim if we hold onto the side of the pool. We must let go of the negative thoughts, ideas, and concepts that are stopping us. I remember when I first started to speak professionally; someone asked me, "Who wants to listen to you, and what do you really have to say?" These words echoed in my head for months, and I sat on the sidelines.

Let go of the fears, worries, and doubts. If you have to write them down on a piece of paper and burn them, do it. Have a funeral for your fears, worries, and doubts. Let them rest in peace so that you can live, work, and play in peace.

34 Why Do You Want What You Want?

We must understand what we want because what we want is the motive behind our motivation, the drive behind our dreams, and the power that fuels the possibilities. Many people think they want something, but they don't know why.

If we understand what we want and why we want it, it will make obtaining it much easier, more rewarding, and more satisfying. If we know why we want something, overcoming the problems and obstacles will not be as confusing. When we understand our wants, we have reasons that lead us to results. If we do not understand them, they are simply wishes or hopes. I once heard a radio announcer say, "If wishes were horses, beggars would ride."

When I was in Washington on a trip with some young adults at a conference, one of the girls called her parents and complained that she did not have enough freedom to travel throughout the hotel. Her parents contacted the trip coordinator and asked if their child could have some freedom to travel independently. The parents also insisted that the child not know that the conversation had taken place with the coordinator. "We want our child to feel free," the parents explained. "If she knew we called, she would feel embarrassed."

The trip coordinators discussed the matter and decided to let the girl have some freedom for the afternoon. They had a brief conversation with the young lady, and she was glad to know that the group leaders had enough confidence in her to give her some freedom in the hotel.

After lunch, some activities were scheduled. Some people went to the game room, and some spent time with friends. The young lady who wanted the freedom only took a nap. She did not need special permission and extra freedom in the hotel to take a nap. Some people like to complain, some people like to criticize, and some people like to make excuses about why they are not having fun.

Don't ask for freedom and then only take a nap. Use your freedom to learn, explore, and live. When we know why we are doing something, it's not as easy to give up when a problem comes. When we have a M.A.P. — a Mission and A Purpose — the flame will not go out when the winds of discouragement start to blow. The desire will not be lost, and the battles can be fought without losing enthusiasm.

Many people ask for a lot and don't even want what they ask for. Others go to the ocean of life with a teaspoon or an eyedropper. They demand nothing from life or from themselves. When we understand why we want something, fear and doubt will still show up, but we have the courage, momentum, and reasons to overcome the resistance.

35 The Best Thing We Can Pay: *Attention*

Do you remember reading Aesop's fable about the goose that laid the golden egg? There was a farmer who was just making ends meet. One day he found a golden egg near his goose. He thought someone was trying to play a trick on him, so he tossed the egg into the bushes. He then thought about it and decided to have the egg appraised. It was solid gold. The day after that, another golden egg appeared; in fact, another golden egg appeared each day. The farmer became rich, and then he became greedy. He decided that he wanted all the eggs right away, so he chopped off the goose's head. Then he reached inside and found . . . nothing. He destroyed the thing that made him rich.

What is your goose with golden eggs? Are you taking care of the goose? Are you letting the goose work extremely hard without any encouragement or relaxation time? If the goose doesn't have the chance to relax, it just may get fed up and find someone else to work with.

I think of the goose as our strengths, talents, and abilities. One day when we pass from this life to another, we will meet our Creator, and He will say, "I gave you many skills, talents, abilities. Did you use them to their greatest potential?"

I want to make sure that I am able to confidently reply, "Yes, I did."

If we continue to shove our dreams and strengths to the back burner, we hold back how our life is truly supposed to be. We spend more time, money, and energy on treatments than on prevention.

Do not confuse research with procrastination. Procrastination is getting ready to be ready. We can spend more time doing the research than it would take us to complete the task. I believe this is equivalent of not feeding the golden goose. If you spend time getting ready to be perfect and do not start out to accomplish your dreams, you will find out later that you could have accomplished your dream if you had just acted.

We must put the emphasis on today, not tomorrow. We must put our dreams in motion today. The word *hesitate* starts with *he* and contains the word *sit*. We cannot hesitate. We must act. We must focus on the golden goose, take great care of it, and give it love. Give it the opportunity to grow, live, and become. Give yourself the opportunity to become.

36 Get Your Dreams Moving!

I once heard someone say that no one will take care of our dreams as well as we will. And really others shouldn't take care of our dreams because they are ours; we should take care of them. People are busy accomplishing their own dreams, so your dreams are left up to you. When you *decide* — that's a key word — to take care of your dreams, things start to happen.

A supervisor met individually with all his employees. After one of the meetings, the supervisor gave his employee a round, wooden coin with the letters t-o-i-t. The employee thanked his boss for the gift and proceeded to ask what it symbolized. The supervisor quickly replied, "You're always saying you're going to get around to it."

Don't just say or think you're going to get around to it, but get to work on your dreams and plans. If you aim for nothing, you'll hit it right on the head, and if you aim for something, you will hit that too. Today, for whatever activity you are going to begin, ask this question: "Will this bring me closer to my dreams or farther away from them?" Invest your time and energy in activities that will leave you fulfilled, not drained.

Our focus is our future, and what we focus on will multiply in our life. Develop the habit of focusing on the possibilities, not the problems. I know people who seem to have a Ph.D. in worry. If they don't have a problem to worry about, they are worrying about the problems that might show up.

When we are solution-minded and when we work, live, and act with faith, the solutions will come our way. Don't just *wait* around. *Get* around to living your dreams.

Part VI
Believing

37 Fear Not!

Don't be afraid. I know that's easier said than done. I learned this lesson when I was on a scout camping trip in the sixth grade. One of my favorite things to do even today is to go camping with family and friends. As a side note, I believe camping equipment is one of the best family gifts parents can give to their children. Camping is something the whole family can do together. It is lots of fun, and it teaches teamwork and organizational skills.

I was encouraged by my parents to go on the scout camping trip at a Boy Scout campsite called Glen Gray in Oakland, New Jersey. I'm not sure if they wanted to get rid of me for the weekend or if they knew it would be a character-building experience, but if you've never been camping with a bunch of ten- and eleven-year-olds, it is an experience you'll never forget.

Camping teaches us many valuable lessons, like being a good planner. One needs to be a good planner to plan meals, plan proper clothing for the weather, and remember first-aid supplies. Sitting around a campfire at night is a great way to get to know each other. There are no phones, emails, or interruptions, just quality conversations. Camping is liberating. It gets us back to our roots and gives us appreciation for the hot, running water and electricity we take for granted every day.

I loved camping with the Boy Scouts because many, if not all, tasks were done with another person or the entire troop. As a blind child, doing things alone in an unfamiliar surrounding was scary. Tasks like collecting wood, getting water from the well, patrolling the campsite for litter, and cooking was always done as a group.

One of the greatest challenges I found when camping was hiking on trails. Trails were not straight or flat. There were brush, rocks, and fallen trees to climb over. There were puddles as big as small rivers and plant growth that would snag your pant leg.

Reflecting back, I was too self-conscious to ask for help, so I just listened for the other scouts in front of me to find my way around. The danger of listening for other people is that they aren't always where you want to go. I managed to fumble and bumble my way through the trip, falling several times.

It's hard enough trying to listen to people's voices; add a little fatigue and a thirty-pound backpack, and now you've got some challenges. I fell down several times, cutting my wrists, elbows, knees, the palms of my hands, and even the bridge of my nose from my glasses. I was too afraid to have a good time and wondered how angry my parents were going to be when they saw me all banged up. I wondered if I would ever be allowed to go camping again.

Then came Sunday afternoon, and my cuts were bandaged. I finally felt comfortable, and the hurts weren't so bad. It felt so good to laugh when scouts and troop leaders discussed the weekend's events. As we cleaned up, laughed, and ate leftover food, the bumps and bruises didn't seem so important.

We packed up the van to head home from our adventure. As we got closer to the church parking lot, my fears started to build like an internal thermometer rising. I began to wonder what my parents would say. As the van pulled into the parking lot, parents gathered around to help the scouts get out of the van and unload their packs. After the van was unloaded, I saw my mother and father smiling at me. They asked, "Did you have a good time?"

"Yes," I answered with my head down. I started showing them my hands, wrists, and elbows.

My father laughed and said, "Looks like you had a good time."

My mother said, "Your clothes stink like a campfire."

I nervously asked, "You're not mad because I fell down?"

My father replied as we were walking back to the car, "No, because I know you have what it takes to get back up." I was relieved, and I received a great feeling of satisfaction. I remember thinking that they believed in me and that it's okay to fall down because I have what it takes to get back up.

38 What's in the Driver's Seat?

On my seventeenth birthday, I was going to take a ride to the bakery with my brother-in-law to pick up my birthday cake. Before we left, he was joking with my family and said, "David's going to be driving home, so it might take a little while." Everyone began to laugh, including myself, but inside I was crushed, to say the least.

Most of my classmates in high school had already gone for their driver's license. I had heard that driving is freedom and that the word *car* begins the word *career*. The fact that I wasn't driving was a lot to handle. I understood that as a blind person, using public transportation and making use of drivers were things I needed to learn how to manage. I understood that even though I wasn't sitting in the driver's seat, I could still get to where I needed to go. I knew what my choices were.

I have learned that one of two things can be in the driver's seat: faith or fear. If fear drives us, we are being reactive, not pro-active. We are acting out of desperation, not inspiration. F.E.A.R. is False Evidence Appearing Real. My brother Vincent told me that when he was in the army, F.E.A.R. meant Forget Everything And Run. That is the emotion that shows up when you have fear.

If faith is in the driver's seat, we allow our dreams to shine through, the problems don't seem so big, the mountain doesn't seem so large, and the people don't appear so mean. When faith is in the driver's seat, we aren't afraid to ask for help, and we don't sound desperate when asking for the sale. We sound hopeful, not hopeless. No one likes to buy from a desperate salesperson, no one who's discouraged wants to hear a success story, and no one who's full of fear wants to talk about faith. However, the best remedy for fear is faith, the best remedy for discouragement is encouragement plus action, and the best remedy for hopelessness is a powerful dream.

Faith is risking it all on the unseen. Faith means you can live with the uncertainty without breaking down. Faith is the fuel behind all great action, the driving force that will bring you closer to your dreams. I have met so many people who have told me their dreams are dead. Faith can revive our dreams. Faith can bring our dreams off the shelf and back into ourselves. If we just sit around hoping, wishing, and wondering if our dreams will come true, they won't. But if we have a dream and back it with faith and action, mountains will crumble, doors will open, and people will show up to help.

We must be in the driver's seat of our mind. We must drive through the positive thoughts and detour around the negative thoughts. If we allow our mind to stay in neutral and idle on negative fuel, the fears will show up again and again and again. If we put our minds in drive, filling them with positive fuel and the power of a dream, who knows where we can go?

When a plan is in place and faith is applied, our dreams come alive. Today, allow faith to be in the driver's seat so that your family, company, and health can thrive. Remember that you are unstoppable. Keep striving and driving, and your dreams will be alive.

39 The Key Ingredient for Self-Esteem

We can go to bookstores, libraries, and even the Internet to find thousands of books on the subject of building self-esteem. I have spent thousands of hours studying professional athletes, professional entertainers, and top salespeople, and I have found many common threads in their success. I have found that being committed to our commitments and making contributions to our emotional bank accounts are ways to build self-esteem.

When trouble shows up — and it will — how will we react? If we have high self-esteem, we will be confident when the winds of trouble begin to howl. If we are not committed and confident when trouble shows up, we will be quick to give up.

How many times have you said, "I'm going to lose fifteen pounds"? Later that afternoon you eat a burger and super-sized fries. When things aren't going our way, the thought of quitting shows up. We think quitting is the way: quit the diet, quit the class, quit the workout. Quitting always feels good temporarily. When you think of quitting, have the will to hang in there for another few minutes. When we are committed to our commitments, we know that whatever the problem, whatever the challenge, whatever the obstacle, we have the inner strength to handle it.

I remember being at East Stroudsburg University and training for a power-lifting contest with my fraternity brother Glen Batson (Chicken Hawk). I was training for the 132-pound weight class, and I weighed 146 pounds. I had to lose fourteen pounds in just a few months.

This was not a huge task, but I was already at eight percent body fat. Every night Glen and I would train for two hours and then have dinner in the college cafeteria. While standing in line, Glen would say, "David, I don't know if you are going to believe this, but they have nothing to eat tonight but salad." I knew this was not true because I could smell the other food cooking. Glen knew what I must eat. Real friends will help us stay committed.

A week before the contest, some individuals said, "Dave, come eat. You'll never lose the weight. You don't have what it takes to lose it." People who try to coax us away from our dreams are not our friends. We must spend time with individuals who will help us keep our commitments. Thanks to the support of my friends, I was able to make the 132-pound weight class by the morning of the contest.

If we are going to build self-esteem, we must get committed to our promises to ourselves and to others. We must not be wishy-washy. We must not think, "Why bother? I never stay on the diet." If we cannot control our desires and urges, they will rule us.

When I was knee high to a grasshopper, my Aunt Rose told me not to make promises I couldn't keep to a child. She went on to explain that adults will forgive and forget, but kids never forget. Do not dwell on the past or on the commitments you've broken in the past. Focus on the moment at hand, for that is the moment of potential weakness and the moment of potential strength.

Spend time with people who keep their word to themselves and to others. Forbidden fruit creates a jam. Stay away from forbidden fruit, keep your commitments, and nourish your mind with positive information. Then you will continue to develop self-esteem, and you will be a positive example from which others can learn.

40 Potential: What It Really Means

I am not a big movie fan, but a movie I really enjoyed was *A Bronx Tale* with Robert DeNiro. My favorite line in that movie is "There's nothing worse than wasted potential." That line really spoke to me. We have skills, talents, and abilities deep inside of us, and all we have to do is take the time to bring them out. We also have feelings inside us that we don't know about. I experienced this when Mariann and I had our son David Junior. Emotions came out that we never knew we had, but they were always inside us. We have to have the courage, time, and patience to bring them out. We also have a champion inside us that hard work, determination, and a red-hot, burning desire will bring out.

While attending public school, I spent one period each day in the resource room. This special education classroom was a place I could go to get help with any work that was assigned. I remember feeling that because I was in special education classes, some teachers didn't expect much from me. Some teachers thought that if students were in special education, they were limited in what they could do. But special education is filled with students who have many different abilities and learning styles.

There was a girl in special classes who was severely physically disabled, but she was allowed to take art with the other students. While in art class, each student was given a ball of clay. Some students made cups, some students made ashtrays, and some students made plaques. No one, including the teacher, was paying any attention to the disabled student. As the teacher started cleaning up, she walked past the young disabled student and was amazed at the beautiful statute the girl had sculpted. The teacher said, "Please show the rest of the class."

The young girl struggled to raise the statute; it was an Olympic champion with arms raised in victory. The student asked the class, "Do you know what it is? It is a champion." Then she dropped the artwork to the table and started rolling it into a ball in her hands. She then raised the ball of clay into the air and asked the class, "Do you know what it is now? It is a hidden champion."

I truly believe that there is a hidden champion inside all of us, and we must have the courage to bring it out. Yes, we must face doubt. Yes, we must take risks. Yes, we will fail at times. If we never believe, we will never achieve. Today take the time to bring out the God-given skills inside you, and make this world a better place for your family, friends, and everyone else.

41 The First Lesson I Learned in College

I attended East Stroudsburg University in Pennsylvania. My first class was on Monday morning at eight—Introduction to Philosophy with Dr. Eshelmen. He came into the room and began to write on the blackboard. When he finished, he turned around and said, "Learn this." The words on the board were "Without pleasure you will not understand pain, and without pain you will not understand pleasure." I've heard someone say that God lets us experience pain so we don't forget we're alive.

That first class had a lasting impression on me. I always wondered why we have problems, and that was the answer. "Without pleasure we will not understand pain." I've always tried to avoid pain, but that is not realistic. I also do not recommend going around looking for pain because at some point the messenger of misery will always find us and knock on our door.

This may sound gory, but it's true. I do, however, believe that every problem comes bearing a gift. Sometimes the gift is an opportunity to get in touch with our feelings, or it could be something else altogether. Whatever the case may be, don't lose sight of the lesson each and every problem brings.

I think one of the deepest pains we can encounter is the break up of a relationship. When people tell us that they are going to leave us because they are in love with someone else or it's just not working out, it can be devastating. The numbing pain of this seems unbearable at times, but this empty, lonely, helpless feeling will pass. We grow stronger from these experiences and will be able to create healthier, more meaningful relationships in the future.

One of the greatest pains I personally encountered was when I couldn't see myself in the mirror anymore. This happened when I was about eighteen-years-old and had just started college. I knew something was wrong, but denial is a big river. I blamed the problem on poor lighting, a change in vitamins, or any other ridiculous theory I could conjure up.

The pain, frustration, and despair were simply an opportunity for me to take a good look at myself on the inside and see myself from an entirely different perspective. The harder I tried to be like everyone else, the more foolish I looked. Until we realize that we are all individuals with our own special gifts, talents, and abilities, we will not realize pleasure. When we swim around in "keeping up with the Joneses" and trying to be like everyone else, internal pain will persist; it will always be there. But when we allow ourselves to be who we really are, pleasure begins to flow from us like a great gusher.

When we try to change ourselves because we think someone else will like us more, we just fool ourselves. When we are true to ourselves, we feel free, liberated from the changes of doubt and fear. We must be true to ourselves, and peace will flow.

Pleasure and pain are two of the greatest driving forces. Pain can drive us to making decisions that we will contemplate for years to come. Pleasure will drive us to making decisions that will be memorable. I remember when I first met Mariann, and my friends would ask me what she was like. I told them she was funny, caring, and smart. The only problem with her was that she was too nice, I said. Imagine that. I was concerned that she was too nice. I found out later that that is one of the greatest attributes a person can have.

Today, learn from the pain, learn the lessons, and look for the opportunities. Pleasure will come when you allow yourself to be yourself. Start from the inside and take off that internal mask you've been wearing. Be yourself for a change. Don't worry about the outside and what other people might think. If you become who you desire to become on the inside, the outside will take care of itself. You were born an original; don't die a duplicate.

Part VII
Persevering

42 A Lesson from the First Grade

One of the first lessons I learned in school was that everyone gets a turn. I remember feeling inferior because I couldn't run as fast as the other kids could. I mean I could run fast, but I didn't in order to avoid running into a tree, a pole, or anything else. I would always run with my brakes on and follow the other kids' voices. I remember feeling sick whenever I heard, "Last one there is a rotten egg." Yes, I was always the last one there, and yes, I was always laughed at because I was the rotten egg.

I never realized how bad getting laughed at hurt until I was in seventh grade. It was my first day in Belleville Middle School, and we students were given a three-by-five card on which to write our name, address, parents' names, and phone number. I couldn't see the lines, so I had no idea where to write. I asked a girl next to me if she could please help me and write the information on the card. She started to laugh and then told her friend. They both started to laugh. My stomach dropped, and I thought I was going to throw up. The other girl asked, "What's wrong with you anyway?" They both started to laugh. I felt horrible and helpless.

Holding back tears, I tried to print my name and address. When the bell rang, I brought the card to the teacher. I was going to explain that I was legally blind and used Braille. I handed him the card and started to explain, "My name is David De Notaris, and I am . . ."

"Young man," the teacher interrupted, "if you think you are going to write like this in my class, you are mistaken."

"I am blind and use Braille to write," I said. Then I heard the sound of the teacher crumpling up the card; it added to the pathetic feeling I had.

"You're blind?" he asked.

"Yes," I replied.

"You'd better run along to your next class before you are late."

Finally, the end of the day arrived, and I could go home. I was never so happy to go home. All I had to do was figure out which of the four buses was mine. I asked the first bus driver if this was the correct bus. We had been told that we would have the same bus driver in the morning and in the afternoon. The bus driver said sarcastically, "Was I your bus driver this morning?"

"I can't see," I replied. "I don't remember."

She said, "Nope, this is not your bus." I went to the second, third, and fourth bus and asked where they were going, but none were going to my stop. Eventually, there were no kids left on the sidewalk, and the buses were getting ready to leave.

I ran up to the first bus again and asked, "Where do you stop?"

Before the bus driver could respond, one of my friends shouted, "Get on before you miss the bus!" I was relieved. I felt like I was living some kind of sick joke, but I was relieved that I was finally on my way home.

I walked in the door, and my mother asked, "David, how was your first day?"

"Fine, I am going to watch TV." It never felt so good to just sit on the floor in my house, and I fell asleep. Two hours later my father came home from work with a big watermelon, my favorite fruit.

He asked, "David, how was your first day at school?"

I broke down crying. "Horrible, Dad, it was horrible. Kids laughed at me, and I couldn't find the bus. I thought I was going to be left at school."

My father hadn't started eating dinner yet, and he said, "Come on, David, we are going to go in the yard."

My mother said, "But dinner is going to get cold."

"That's okay," my father said. We went in the yard, and my father made me start doing push-ups and sit-ups. Then he took the watermelon and made me press it over my head.

My mother asked from the kitchen window, "What are you doing?"

My father replied, "I am helping our son get his self-confidence back." That night my father assured me that he would take care of everything, and that is what he did.

The next morning he took me to school, and we met with the principal. My father explained the story. Mr. DeMaggio was very upset and said, "David, I am sorry. I will fix everything." He instructed my father to take me home. I would come back on Monday morning.

I am not sure what my father and Mr. DeMaggio did, but everything worked out. Mr. DeMaggio also reminded me of the lesson I learned back in first grade. He said, "David, I am sorry you had some problems your first day, but everyone gets a turn to win, lose, and get laughed at."

It's true. We all get a turn to win, lose, and get laughed at. What turn are you taking today? Whatever the turn, remember the feeling associated with your turn so that you can share it with someone else. Feel the pleasure, feel the pain, and remember that we are never given a load we can't carry. So keep hoping, keep praying, keep moving your feet, and never, never, never give up.

43 Out of Sorts

Have you ever said or heard anyone say, "I feel out of sorts"? We feel out of sorts when we are going through life without a plan. We go to work or to the gym or to the store without knowing why we are there, but we are there. We question ourselves, wondering what we are doing. We really should be doing something else. When we are at work, we are thinking about home. When we are at the gym, we are thinking about work. When we are at home, we are thinking about work and the gym. This out-of-sorts feeling shows up when there is the absence of an organized plan. This isn't necessarily a bad thing; however, it will cause discomfort.

The good news about feeling out of sorts is that our body is letting us know that changes are about to take place. The changes may be growing pains. Maybe we are growing out of a job or out of our circle of friends. It can mean that our friends or co-workers are not satisfied with our behavior, and maybe our actions should be modified. Someone once said that the only kind of change that people like is the kind that's in their pockets.

Feeling out of sorts may just mean you need a hug from your husband, wife, child, or good friend. How do you know when you're feeling out of sorts? One way is feeling like you woke up with a giant question mark over your bed. You feel like everything is some type of question or sick riddle. We wonder, "Why did she say that? What did she mean by that? Was I supposed to take that comment another way? Why aren't they returning my calls or emails?" Other thoughts include "The hell with it. Why bother? Who needs them anyway? If she's going to act that way, then I'll do it anyway."

Feeling out of sorts means something that is altering our mood has entered our environment. It could be drugs, alcohol, another person, more responsibilities, work, fear about money, our family, or friends. When we feel out of sorts, we think of the ten most damaging words in the world: What will other people say? What will other people think?

The funny thing about these words is that people really don't care what you do because they are too preoccupied with figuring out what they themselves are doing. Feeling out of sorts may mean you are thinking negative thoughts about yourself or others.

I remember being in first grade and learning Braille while the other kids were learning the print alphabet. I felt left out, as if I were apart from the class and not a part of the class. I was very upset, and Mrs. Higgins asked me what was wrong. I guess six-year-olds aren't very hard to read. I told her I wanted to learn print like everyone else and not those dots. She kneeled down next to me and said, "David, it doesn't matter how you get the information. What matters is that you get the information." I went from feeling out of sorts to back in the game.

Feeling out of sorts may mean that you haven't had good quality time with a family member or a good friend from high school or college. I know when I feel down, I can always call my friend Chris. Chris can always make me laugh and make me look at a situation with another perspective. This always makes me feel a lot lighter, not in weight but in the heart. We put so much pressure on ourselves to always keep up with the Joneses. We pressure ourselves to believe we should have what other people have and be whatever they are. When we sit back and think about what they have, sometimes we really don't even want it.

The remedy for feeling out of sorts is getting an organized plan. You need to figure out the type of person that you want to become and stop trying to be someone else. Don't worry about your past failures; just chalk them up to learning experiences and move on! You see, we cannot live in the past; however, we must learn from the past. Stop the destructive disaster thinking and get down to the business of making an organized plan for your life because that's what you have control over.

You have control over your thoughts, and unless you take control of them, they will take control of you. You have the most powerful, wonderful, and creative computer on your shoulders. Use it to design the kind of life you desire. When you feel out of sorts, just remember the song that says, "Pick yourself up, dust yourself off, and start all over again." You'll start feeling like yourself because you have a plan, and most important, you will get in motion.

44 Overcoming Fatigue Every Day

Overcoming fatigue is not always easy; however, it is possible. The great football coach Vince Lombardi said, "Nothing makes cowards of men like fatigue." Fatigue blurs one's thinking, vision, planning, and evaluating. Fatigue causes individuals to make poor choices, choosing either the easy way out or not trying at all. Behavior resulting from fatigue can leave us wondering, "What was I thinking? Was I thinking when I made that decision?" Today in our world of instant messaging, personal data systems, and movies on demand, we have the ability to make decisions that are immediately fulfilled.

The danger that lies within this immediate fulfillment is acting within the moment without thinking of the consequences. For example, let's say that you are angry with someone. You decide to write a letter to explain your anger. You put it in an envelope, seal the envelope, and leave it on your desk to mail the next day. After you put it on the desk, you may wake up the next morning and say, "Forget it; they aren't worth it anyway." Then you could throw the letter into the garbage, never exposing yourself or your emotions to someone who may have hurt you. However, today with our modern technology, we could write the same letter out of anger, frustration, or unclear thinking (fatigue); then we could fax or email the letter.

Fatigue causes us to say things we wouldn't under normal circumstances. We all know the saying "Once the bottle is spilled, you can never get all the water back in." In other words, once the words are out there, even "I'm sorry" can't repair all the damage.

A first step in overcoming fatigue is realizing that we are feeling fatigued. In our fast-paced world, everyone is in a rush to get the job done. It amazes me that today with our faster cars, computers, and research, people seem to have less and less time to do the things they love to do.

A second way to overcome fatigue is to give yourself more time to do things you love to do. In my seminars, I ask people to think of the things that they love to do. I ask seminar participants to make a list of the things they love to do: play golf, walk on the beach, fish, shop, play with their kids, go to a ball game. Once that list is complete, I tell everyone to stand up and think how excited they are going to feel knowing they're going to do what they love to do.

Imagine yourself doing what is on your list. How happy do you feel?

I then ask what sound people would put with that emotion. This always gets some chuckles. I then ask them to imagine doing what they love, raise their arms up in the air, make the sound associated with what they love to do, and shout it as loud as they can. This is the best fatigue buster I have ever found. People always laugh at first; then some people yell "four" as if they were playing golf. Some people yell "half-price sale," and some people yell "home run," whatever they associate with pleasure.

Fatigue comes not just from being tired but also from not doing what you need to and love to do for yourself. Today make the time to spend time with yourself and figure out the things you need to do with yourself and others.

Another fatigue buster is making a list. This may sound simple, but few people do it. Many people are carrying around their "To Do" list in their head rather than in a notebook or day planner. William James said, "Nothing is more mentally fatiguing than holding onto the uncompleted task." So as we know, once again, it's all in our head. Get it out of your head and put it on paper. You'll feel better, lighter, even faster. I have a good friend who told me that he would rather have a short pencil than a long memory.

Fatigue can hold you down, even cause physical or mental sickness, so take the simple suggestions given in this chapter and give yourself more energy, more fun, and more satisfaction. You'll feel better for it.

45 Problems Are Your Promotions.

What are you going to do when the storm comes? When I talk about storms, I am not talking about rain, tornadoes, or hurricanes. I am talking about the emotional ones: the storms of rejection, the storms of fear, the storms of regret, and the storms of failure. The neurological storms that happen to every one of us are known as life.

I can remember back to when I was a sophomore in college at East Stroudsburg University and was pledging to a national fraternity, Phi Sigma Kappa. I believe this was one of the greatest experiences I ever had.

Pledging kept us very busy. Spending time at the fraternity house; mandatory time at the library doing schoolwork; and time eating, sleeping, and exercising made for some tight schedules. My family wasn't very happy about my pledging to a fraternity. My mother repeatedly asked me, "Do you know what you are doing? Are you sure this is a good idea? How is this going to affect your schoolwork?" It was quite obvious that my family wasn't happy about my activities.

It is hard to feel good about yourself when your family — almost a hundred miles away — is questioning your activities. Now for some windy weather — you can almost hear the wind starting to gust and blow. Mix in my first serious girlfriend, who was less stable then I was, and now we have the ingredients for a wild storm. I had three great pledge brothers: Mike, Shaun, and Dave. We had a lot of fun together. We had been pledging for seven weeks when all the fun and busyness turned to aggravation and exasperation.

Vince Lombardi said, "Fatigue turns men into cowards." That is what I turned into: a coward. So many things were on my mind: my grades, my family, and the fraternity.

It was Sunday afternoon. I finished washing and folding my laundry. I finished studying for my school and fraternity test, and I was going to — I hoped — take a two-hour Sunday nap. I snuggled up in my fuzzy blanket and listened to the football game while I peacefully fell asleep. Then I was awakened by a knock at my door. It was my girlfriend. I was happy to see her even though we had been fighting on and off. She hit me with an old tomato; I mean an ultimatum. "It's the fraternity or me," she explained.

I was a wreck. I really thought I was in a nightmare. All I wanted to do was sleep. Just the thought of losing my first girlfriend was murder, even though we really didn't get along well. I was physically sick. I threw up and couldn't catch my breath. I just totally lost it. I said, "You're kidding."

"No," she shouted, "it's me or them! You've changed."

I thought that maybe this was just another fight. My heart started pounding, and my thoughts started racing. How could I live without her? Who will help me? What will I do now? Who will I spend time with? I felt hopeless and helpless. I was in tears. I told her I was sorry for everything and begged her to reconsider.

I didn't understand why I felt this way. We really didn't even have fun together. As a matter of fact, whenever she opened her mouth, she made me nervous. She would fly off the handle at any time. At the drop of a hat, she would flip her lid, and if the hat didn't drop, she would knock it off so that she could flip anyway. I always felt nervous, uneasy, and even sick.

I didn't know what to do. This was the first time I ever learned about neurological storms. I would break into cold sweats just sitting on the couch. She was nowhere around, but the thought of her would send a heat-charged chill from the top of my head into my legs. Thank God, I've never had that sensation since.

The torment didn't stop there. After she left my dorm room, she continued to call my dorm, wanting to talk to me, wanting to be friends. I had nothing to say. I knew what I was going to do. I had pledged for seven weeks, and she was not going to stop me from joining the fraternity. She left messages on my answering machine, saying that she hated my guts and that I was a failure and that I didn't deserve to go out with her.

Then she started writing letters. My roommates would read them to me, and the letters were even crazier then her phone messages. I remember my roommate Mike reading me a letter she wrote. He opened the letter, began reading it, and then crumbled it up. "Dave, it's not worth reading." Then he threw it out.

"Come on, Mike, just read it, okay?" I asked. He took the letter out of the garbage and unraveled it.

"Dave, you don't want to hear this," Mike pleaded.

But I replied, "Just go on."

The letter said, "Dear Dave, I can't go out with you anymore because you're blind. My family says you'll never amount to anything, and I am breaking up with you to go out with someone else. P.S. I hope God heals your eyes because you are a nice person. Love . . . ."

This letter was not an emotional storm but a title wave. Emotions came over me. I don't remember what happened after I finished throwing up, but the hot and cold sweats continued for three weeks.

In our lives we all come to a turning point, and mine came in my fraternity house when a brother, Tom Barnic, said to me while I was still pledging, "Dave, I know you're going through some stuff, but the brothers are behind you one hundred percent. You're going to make it." It felt so good; that was the encouragement I needed. He explained this to me while I was mopping the kitchen floor. He opened up to me about a girl who had broken up with him. It felt good knowing someone else had felt some of what I was going through.

I completed pledging and became a brother. Looking back on the situation, I think sleep depravation may have played a part in all of my feelings, but it was a crazy scene, nonetheless. When facing a neurological storm, it's never the time to make a life-changing decision to call it quits, but it's a time to look to God, family, and friends to support you.

Another lesson I learned during this difficult time is only share your heartbreaks and your dreams with people who are going to encourage you. I remember one of the hurts I felt when going through this college breakup was one of my family members saying to me, "You'd better do whatever she wants because how many people want to marry or just be with a blind person?" It seems to me that families always know what buttons to push.

Please only share your dreams with individuals who are encouraging, who are in accord with you. Share your dreams with people who are like-minded, who will *help you figure out how* and *not ask you how* you are going to do it. When a storm comes and the wind starts to blow, we must protect ourselves by surrounding ourselves with solid family and friends. When we do this the torrential storms will come, and we will stand tall, remain calm on the inside, be strong on the outside, and emerge victoriously.

46 A Gray Day

I don't have many of them, but when they show up, boy, are they yucky. Are you having a gray day today? Are you letting life's problems get you down? It happens to everyone. There is no secret for facing a gray day, but here are some ideas that will make it a little brighter.

1. Look to heaven and say, "Lord, please see me through this one!" That helps take the focus off me. I have sat and wasted many hours wondering, "Why me?" It doesn't help to sit and mope. Look for hope.

2. Keep your chin up. You may have heard this before, but do you know why it really works? When we keep our chin up, we take in more oxygen, and oxygen promotes healing. Think of this quote: "If you can look up, you can get up!"

3. Count your blessings and be grateful for the things you have, the people that you know, and the person you are. Success isn't getting what you want but wanting what you have.

4. Identify why you are feeling gray. Maybe you must "H.A.L.T." because you are hungry, angry, lonely, or tired.

5. Go get a little success. Do something you like to do or something you do well: walking around the block, reading a book, or listening to music.

Dale Carnegie said, "Worry comes from the lack of an organized plan." If you are not gray today, be thankful. Take this time to identify the things that would psych you up if you were gray.

Maybe a storm is overhead, maybe it just left, or maybe it's on the way. Whatever the challenge, setback, or dilemma, ask God to see you through. Keep your chin up, count your blessings, figure out the problem, and go make something great happen. You can do it. Start now. Shake off the gray, and make this your day.

47 If It Doesn't Kill You, It Will Make You Stronger.

The first time I heard this proverb I was in college at East Stroudsburg University. I was feeling sorry for myself and complaining about all the things that I had to do that the other students didn't have to do. For example, I had to hire readers to read to me the books I couldn't get on tape.

My roommate Mike was a very nice guy and said, "David, if it doesn't kill you, it will make you stronger." I guess he was tired of my complaining. He told me to just "get it done because complaining isn't going to help."

I remember taking a deep breath and saying, "Fine, I'll do it." I didn't want to do it, but I knew I had to; my college education depended on it. Today the skills I learned while recruiting, interviewing, and hiring readers still help me. The skills I learned can apply to any management position.

1. Planning. We must answer these questions: What do I need? Where can I find it?
2. Organizing. We must clearly organize our thoughts and develop a written action plan with a specific timeline for completion.
3. Staffing. As the managers of our lives, we must know what the job is that we are filling and what the skills are that we need to do the job well. When I was hiring a reader for science courses, I would look for someone with a science background to explain scientific equations and formulas.
4. Delegating. No one can do everything, so we must look to see what people like to do. I have learned that people always excel in things they like to do. Some people are good readers but poor researchers. Some people are good report writers, and others take wonderful notes. I learned the 3D principle: Do it, delegate it, or dump it.
5. Supervising. We must first be able to manage ourselves before we can manage anyone else. We must make sure our staff is aware of deadlines and responsibilities. We must enroll staff into our vision. Staff members need to know what we want to accomplish and how we are going to do it.
6. Evaluating. We must be able to put our heads down and work, work, work. We then must

pick our heads up and ask what is working well. What needs improvement? We must build on what is working and modify what isn't.

7. Reporting. We must be able to report in print. Always leave a paper trail. We must also report verbally so that we can articulate to our boss or spouse how resources are being spent.

I remember sitting in my dorm room, agonizing over the problems of recruiting, interviewing, hiring, training, and working with readers. Now I realize that this problem has helped shape the person I am today.

Someone once told me that God lets us have problems so that we don't forget we are alive. The problems we have had shaped the person we are today. Don't say, "I wish I didn't have this problem." Instead ask the question, "What can I learn from this problem?"

Then we can share the problem and the solution with others.

48 Risks: Great Learning Tools

I love this quote: "People who are successful risk something, and those who don't gain nothing." I am not suggesting for one minute that you bet all your money in Atlantic City. I do believe we must risk to dream, then risk to plan, and then risk to act.

The president of a major corporation was asked the secret of becoming more successful. His response was "double your failures." Many people think that risk is failure, and at times it is. However, failures give us more information to work with. If we hold onto the side of the pool, we will never learn to swim. Dale Carnegie said, "Today is the tomorrow we feared yesterday."

We must first risk the time to dream about the person we want to become. We must then identify the risks we will encounter: education, job interviews, business proposals, a date. We must then risk acting on our plan. This is where risk and fear meet to try to knock us off our feet. This is when we must be strong and have faith in the unseen.

Acting on our dreams is the best thing we can do. Many people go to a job or a class or a place, and they dislike or even hate it because they are afraid to risk and change. I heard someone once say some people are happier with the hell they know than the heaven they don't. I believe we have been put here to make a positive difference, and a motto I learned in Boy Scouts is "Leave the site better than you found it." If we are living with regret or anger, we cannot improve anything. When we are dreaming, risking, and growing, we become leaders.

Risk takers have bigger personal networks, are aware of more supports and services, and have an open mind to possibilities. Hockey great Wayne Gretsky said, "We miss one hundred percent of the shots we never take." Today, take a shot. Dream about the person you want to become. Dream about the lessons you must learn, the obstacles you must overcome, and the barriers you must break down. Take the chance and design a POA (plan of action) and a deadline. Take a risk and challenge yourself to become the best person you can become.

49 You Must Remember This. . .

How many times have you set out with a new project, idea, or dream, but months, weeks, or even days later it sputtered, puttered, and then fizzled out? You were left scratching your head, wondering what happened. Where did all the enthusiasm go? You wonder, "What was I thinking when I started?" This has happened to me more times than I'd like to remember. We start out with such high hopes, great dreams, and wonderful intentions, only to find them sitting on the sidelines.

I have found that the most effective tool to combat the problem of DFO (dream fizzle out) is creating reminders. When we set little reminders, they can make a big difference. A reminder can be written on the back of a business card and put in a spot where we can access it easily: the alarm-clock, the bathroom mirror, the refrigerator door, the dashboard of our car, or the monitor of our computer. Our focus is our future. If we focus on all the things we can't do, the number of things we can't do will grow. If we focus on our dreams, they will grow also.

A reminder must be short but specific. We must be clear; that's why a small piece of paper like a business card is perfect. Write the specific action you want to remind yourself to take. It could be just a short statement: I am great at asking for referrals. I eat healthy food. I encourage others. Fill your mind with what you want, so when the storms of life come along and shake you up, you will spill over with confidence, not crumble under the pressure and confusion.

We must remind ourselves that we can do it, that we deserve it, and that we are not afraid. We are always reminding ourselves of something. The reminders come from years of education. Whenever we bounce a check, we remind ourselves that our math teacher told us that we stink at subtracting. Whenever we go off the diet, we remind ourselves that our aunt told us that we have no self-control. When we break something, we remind ourselves that our grandfather told us that we were like a bull in a china shop. However, we need to focus on reminding ourselves of the positive things.

We need to remind ourselves that we are sharp, quick on our feet, always ready to help. Remind yourself that you are a go-getter and a go-giver. Remind yourself that you say what you mean and mean what you say.

We become what we think about, so don't think about all your shortcomings. Everyone has them. Remind yourself that you are a positive person whom people like to be around. Remind yourself that you can and you will. If you remind yourself that you can't, you won't. It's up to you to remember. Develop the habit of remembering the person you desire to be. Set a reminder.

And let me remind you that you can do it.

10 Tips to Stop Whining and Start Winning

1. Know when you're whining and decide to stop.
2. Create a mission.
3. Set goals.
4. Write down your goals.
5. Become unstoppable.
6. Take action; take risks.
7. Believe in what you're doing.
8. Have a can-do attitude.
9. Be focused.
10. Conquer fatigue.

(Courtesy of Mark Riesenberg, a time-management and goal-setting expert and a close friend of mine)

The Three Plus Power Formula for Success

1. Take fifteen to thirty minutes once a month to write down your upcoming month's goals.
2. Take five to ten minutes in the early evening to write down your priorities for the next day.
3. Identify your top three time wasters, and implement a plan to minimize and eliminate them. Note: A time waster switches your attention from a high priority task to a low priority task.
Plus: Have a coach. Everybody needs a coach to maximize potential.

(Courtesy of Mark Riesenberg, a time-management and goal-setting expert and a close friend of mine)